RELISH
MERSEYSIDE
& LANCASHIRE

Original recipes from the region's finest chefs

First Published 2011
By Relish Publications
Shield Green Farm, Tritlington,
Northumberland NE61 3DX

ISBN 978-0-9564205-6-5

Publisher: Duncan L Peters
General Manager: Teresa Peters
Marketing and Design: Ria Parkin
Photography: Tim Green
Proof Assistant: Jack Bamber
Printed By: Balto Print Ltd, Stratford,
London E15 2TF

RELISH
PUBLICATIONS.CO.UK

004
CONTENTS

PAGE	STARTERS	MAINS
010-019	Seafood Tapas	Pan Fried Pork Belly with Butternut Squash Puree, Creamed Mashed Potato and Cider Sauce
020-029	Goosnargh Duck Cottage Pie	Wild Sea Bass Wrapped in Potato with Samphire, Peas, Beans & Pancetta
030-039	Melon, Cured Ham, Creamed Goat's Cheese, Peas & Rapeseed Oil	Halibut with Crab Potatoes & Asparagus
040-049	Pan Fried Hand Dived Scallops, with Pancetta, Black Pudding, Pea and Red Pepper Puree	Sweet and Sour Seabass with Pineapple, Crab and Baby Carrots
050-059	Bouillabaisse	Assiette of Rabbit
060-069	Ham Hock and Tarragon Terrine, Home Smoked Pancetta, Black Pudding Bon Bons, Pea and White Truffle Veloute	Pan Seared Wild Seabass with Morecambe Bay Shrimp, Crab and Chili Ravioli, Oriental Vegetables and Wasabi Hollandaise
070-079	Roasted Butternut Squash, Parmesan Ice Cream and Textures of Woodland Mushroom	Roasted Quail, Beetroot and Truffled Barley
080-089	Tandoori Roast Monkfish – Pig's Trotter Nuggets and Scratching, Sweet Potato, Apple and Cumin	Goosnargh Duck – Poached and Roast Breast, Leg Meat Wontons, Beetroot and Orange
090-099	Braised Oxtail, Shallots in Beer, Potato Puree	Rack of Lonk Lamb, Lamb Breast, Tomato and Cumin, Anna Potatoes
100-109	Spider Crab Salad , Tomato Jelly, Cured Cucumber and Avocado Mousse	Herb Crusted Spring Lamb, Braised New Season Onion Stuffed with Offal, Ratatouille and Red Wine Jus
110-119	Cured Salmon, Jersey Royal Potatoes & 55 Minute Egg Yolk	Fillet of Brill, Wild Mushrooms, Wirral Oxtail & Parsley Pearls

DESERTS

Three Millstones Plate of Desserts

Elderflower Jelly & Panna Cotta with Claremont Farm Strawberries

Set Vanilla Yoghurt with Boozy Strawberries, Shortbread and Black Pepper Caramel

Tiramisu

Crème Brulée with Pimms no. 1 Sorbet and Mint Jelly

Strawberry Textures & Cream

Celery and Rhubarb Sorbet

Mango Ravioli, Rice Pudding and Blood Orange Soup

Vanilla Custard Pots with Lemon Shortbread

Strawberries Delice with Dacquoise Biscuit, Strawberry Jelly and Mousse, White Chocolate and Juniper Ice Cream

Milk Chocolate Mousse, Passion Fruit and Yoghurt Sorbet

RESTAURANTS

	PAGE
3 Millstones Inn	010-019
60 Hope Street	020-029
The Bay Horse Inn	030-039
The Bubble Room	040-049
The Duke of York	050-059
The Fence Gate at Fence	060-069
Fraiche	070-079
Freemasons	080-089
The Inn at Whitewell	090-099
La Mouette at The Royal Hilbre	100-109
The Lawns Restaurant	110-119

006
CONTENTS

PAGE	STARTERS	MAINS
120-129	King scallops with Braised Pork Cheek and Morcilla, Served with Cauliflower Puree, Golden Raisin Dressing and Jus	John Dory with Southport Samphire, Claremont Farm Asparagus, Pommes Violette, Carrot Puree and Crab Bisque
130-139	Ensalada Mariscoa	Ibérico Tender loin with Bubble & Squeak
140-149	Black Pudding, Free Range Egg and Drop Bottom Muffin with Sheeran Brown Sauce	Ballotine of Rabbit with Rabbit Bon Bons, Puy Lentils and Pickled Girolles
150-159	Scottish Smoked Salmon and Mascarpone Cream Cheese Roulade	Pan Roasted Loin of Pork on Carrot Swede and Smoked Bacon Rosti Potato with Wild Mushrooms and Red Wine Sauce
160-169	Spiced Potted Dunsop Bridge Trout, Lemon Jelly, Beer Bread	Hand Raised Bowland Venison Pie, Pilling Samphire, Creamed mash, Bowland Ale Gravy
170-179	Ham, Cheese, Pickle	Shin of Beef
180-189	Ballotine of Chicken, Tarragon and Baby Leeks, Puy Lentil Vinaigrette	Rump of Lamb , Balsamic, Rosemary & Red Onion Marinade, Roasted Garlic Mash, Green Beans
190-199	Confit Salmon, Pickled Cucumber, Salted Cauliflower, Orange, Radish, Shallot	Roasted Pork Belly, Pressed Apple & Raisins, Spiced Carrot Puree, Balsamic Shallots, Pistachio
200-209	Scallops, Spiced Lentils, Pancetta, Wilted Spinach	Pork Cheeks, Morcilla Cannellini Beans
210-219	Grilled Quail with Houmous and Harissa	Roast Cod Fillet with Slow Cooked Fennel, Dill Mash and Southport Shrimp Butter
220-229	Diver Scallops with Black Pudding, Crispy Quail's Eggs, Cauliflower Purée, Red Wine Sauce	Rump of Salt Marsh Lamb, Pastilles of Vegetables, Boulangère Potatoes with Shallot and Mint Confit, Crispy Lamb's Shoulder, Lamb Jus

DESSERTS

Chocolate Marquise with Plum
Sorbet and Chocolate Tuile

Rhubarb and Membrillo Crumble

Tonker Bean Cheese Cake with Salt Caramel and
Poached Peach

Raspberry Mascarpone and White Chocolate
Cheesecake

Kathy's Award Winning Wet Nelly, Custard and
Whipped Cream

Sparkling Elderflower Jelly and
Rose Sorbet

Treacle Tart, Orange Zest Ice Cream

Strawberry & Vanilla Crumble, Clotted Cream
Custard

Dark Chocolate Almond Torte

Rhubarb and Custard Tart

Spiced, Poached Tarporley Rhubarb in Ginger
Crumble, Blackberry and Clove Jelly, Custard Ice
Cream

RESTAURANTS

	PAGE
The London Carriage Works	120-129
Lunya	130-139
Maritime Dining Rooms	140-149
The Monro	150-159
Parkers Arms	160-169
Peninsula Dining Room	170-179
Puschka	180-189
Rhubarb and Custard	190-199
Salt House Tapas	200-209
The Side Door	210-219
Spire	220-229

INTRODUCTION
WITH
PAUL ASKEW

As chairman of the Tourism Business Network and specifically as Food Tourism Champion, Paul is tireless in supporting the North West's local produce determined; to push food tourism to the front of Liverpool's bid to become a truly international destination. He is a member of the Academy of Culinary Arts and enjoys the 'Adopt a School' initiative. As well as his training and mentoring he also works full time in The London Carriage Works kitchen and is the Food and Beverage Director for Hope Street Hotel Ltd. His passion and dedication is an inspiration to those who work with him.

It is a great pleasure to introduce this exciting book. Not only does it show the depth of quality and diversity that our region provides but also the strength and integrity of its Larder.

Chefs and producers have come together in the most amazing way in our region to inspire new dishes and styles of cuisine that fit a very bright new contemporary feel.

Liverpool, once the capital of Lancashire and the Wirral came together in an amazing partnership to make Merseyside a real foodie attraction as you will see from the number of entries in this book from both areas. However we were shown the way by our great Lancastrian trail blazers who opened the doors for this food revolution to happen.

Some thirty years ago I embarked on my gastronomic journey which has taken me across the globe and back to my adopted home city. But what I see now compared to then is truly satisfying. The quality of cooking, the innovation and possibly the most satisfying is the conviviality in the bars, restaurants, cafes and festivals that now exist.

The chefs and restaurants in these pages are all stars of the industry and I applaud every one of them, "the foodie mafia" is growing at a rate of knots in the right direction.

The sommeliers, brewers and wine suppliers have also upped their game and now we are able to create true gastronomy by matching the produce and cooking with great wines and real ales. It is my hope that the book will continue to inspire and define our regional food identity, develop it further and bring more people on the journey to enjoy the magical establishments that the North West provides.

We have all shared some of our recipes and secrets in these chapters and by doing so we hope to inspire our readers to become our clients and guests to join in the celebration of great food, conviviality and of course a legendary warmth of welcome and good humour. So seek out Relish on our proud region and join the revolution.

Paul Askew

010
3 MILLSTONES INN

Waddington Road, West Bradford, Clitheroe, Lancashire BB7 4SX

01200 443 339
www.3millstones.com

The Three Millstones is nestled in the small, picturesque village of West Bradford in the scenic Ribble Valley. The restaurant occupies a beautifully restored, Grade II listed building and is one of the oldest in the village, dating back from the 16th century. Keeping many of its original features, The Millstones offers a blend of the old and new, including traditional flagstone floors, real beams and a magnificent fireplace. The owners, husband and wife team Matthew and Lauren Frost, have been at The Millstones for three years and love the charm and friendliness the restaurant offers. Dining at The Millstones offers a unique, warm and welcoming atmosphere which will make you feel right at home with a professional and charming team to look after you.

Matthew is the restaurant's head chef and has quickly built up an excellent reputation for using local, fresh and seasonal produce, with an ever evolving menu. The menu is a mix of traditional and more contemporary dishes. Matthew can produce exquisite fine dining or dish up some good pub grub. The exceptional food is accompanied by a large wine list and real ales. Our ingredients are always the best; we strive to give our customers freshness and quality.

Dining at the millstones offers a unique, warm and welcoming atmosphere which will make you feel right at home with a professional and charming team to look after you

SEAFOOD TAPAS

SERVES 2

*Kuki Sauvignon Blanc,
Marlborough New Zealand*

Ingredients

Seafood

100g good quality smoked salmon
125g luxury cocktail prawns
125g crayfish tails
2 rollmop herrings

Tempura Batter

100g self raising flour
pinch of salt and sugar
50ml sparkling water
4 Large King Prawns (2 per serving)

Fennel Coleslaw

1 bulb fennel
2 shallots
1 tbsp mayonnaise

chilli sauce
marie rose sauce

Method

For the tempura batter

Place all dry ingredients in a bowl and slowly whisk in the water. Place the peeled prawns in flour then into the batter mix. Lower into the fryer until golden brown.

For fennel coleslaw

Slice a shallot and fennel finely. Combine with mayonnaise.

To serve

Place the other fish onto a plate with the chilli sauce and marie rose as displayed.

PAN FRIED PORK BELLY WITH BUTTERNUT SQUASH PUREE, CREAMED MASHED POTATO AND CIDER SAUCE

SERVES 2

 Carmenere Cabernet Sauvignon, Chile

Ingredients

Pork Belly

½ kg pork belly
2 tbsp rock salt
2 tbsp mixed spices
600ml chicken stock
300ml cider

Butternut Squash

1 butternut squash
100ml double cream

Mashed Potato

2 large Maris Piper potatoes
50g butter

Method

For the pork belly

Rub rock salt and mixed spices into both sides of the pork belly and leave to marinate in the fridge for 24 hours. Once marinated, take the pork belly and wash under a cold tap. Place in warm chicken stock and cider then put into a pre heated oven at 140°C for 3 hours.

For the butternut squash

Whilst the belly is cooking, cut the squash in half, lightly sprinkle it with salt and pepper and place in the oven for 90 minutes. After 90 minutes, take the squash out of the oven and allow to cool for 5 minutes. Then remove all the seeds and scrape out the filling. Place into a blender with the cream and blend for 2-3 minutes.

For the mashed potatoes

Place peeled potatoes in cold, salted water and bring to the boil for 30-40 minutes. Once cooked, remove from water and mash with butter.

For the sauce

Remove the pork belly from the oven, carefully lifting the belly out of the stock. Put the remaining stock and juices into a pan and heat on the hob to make the gravy. Dry the pork belly and place in a medium pre heated ovenproof pan. Then place the pan into a pre heated oven at 200°C, and roast for 20 minutes. This is to crisp the skin.

To serve

When the belly has roasted, place the mashed potato and the puree on a plate then remove the belly, be careful of hot fat spitting. Once the pork stock has reduced by one fifth, drizzle it over the pork, mash and puree and enjoy.

3 MILLSTONES PLATE OF DESSERTS

SERVES 2

 Avondale Late Harvest Muscat

Ingredients

Chocolate Fondant

125g dark chocolate
150g butter
4 egg yolks
2 whole eggs
30g caster sugar
30g cocoa powder
30g plain flour

Mascarpone Meringue

150g egg white
150g caster sugar
150g icing sugar
100g mascarpone cheese
1 vanilla pod

Sticky Toffee Pudding

175g self raising flour
175g dates (chopped)
450ml boiling water
200g soft dark sugar
65g soft butter
2 eggs
1tsp baking powder
1tsp bicarbonate soda

Rhubarb Crumble

100g Yorkshire rhubarb
50g caster sugar
100g plain flour
50g unsalted butter (diced)
50g dark brown sugar

Blackcurrant Parfait

250g fresh blackcurrants (pureed)
100g caster sugar
5 egg yolks
200ml double cream (whipped)

Method

For the chocolate fondant

Melt butter and chocolate together, and whisk in eggs and egg yolks. Then fold in flour and cocoa powder. Pour into moulds and bake for ten minutes at 180°C.

For the mascarpone meringue

Mix egg white with sieved icing and caster sugar, then whisk for ten minutes on a high speed. Place the meringue mix on a tray to approximately 1 inch high, and place in an oven for 1 hour 30 minutes at 100°C. Beat cheese with a split vanilla pod and add to the bottom of the meringue.

For the sticky toffee pudding

Soak dates in hot water. Mix butter and sugar together until creamed. Add flour, bicarbonate soda and baking powder to the sugar and butter mix and then mix them all together. Then add the eggs. Fold in the dates and water. Finally, pour into a baking tray lined with greaseproof paper and bake at 160°C for 30 minutes.

For the rhubarb crumble

Mix sugar and rhubarb together. Place the rhubarb and sugar mixture into a serving dish. Mix flour, sugar and butter together until it looks like breadcrumbs, then place on top of the rhubarb and bake in the oven for 30 minutes at 175°C.

For the blackcurrant parfait

Boil the blackcurrant puree and sugar together. When boiled, slightly cool and pour over whisked egg yolks. Sieve and cool. Once cool, fold the whipped cream and parfait mix together and freeze.

To serve

Assemble as in the picture.

020
60 HOPE STREET

60 Hope Street, Liverpool L1 9BZ

0151 707 6060
www.60hopestreet.com

Renovated and transformed in 1999 by brothers Colin and Gary Manning, this family owned and run restaurant is a hive of culinary activity. 60 is spread over three floors of a Georgian town house in an area rich in history and wonderful architecture. Award-winning for over a decade, their restaurant thrives on a changing menu of seasonal British produce. Now entering its 12th year, 60 Hope Street prides itself on its cuisine and service. Everything on the menu is created with the best quality, seasonal produce, all locally sourced with award-winning seafood from Southport, asparagus from Formby and lamb from Elwy Valley. 60's owners and their team are passionate and committed to providing the best standard of food delivered by an exceptional, unobtrusive level of service. Colin heads the front of house and writes the extensive 60 wine list, whilst Gary leads the way in the kitchen along with design and marketing.

The two brothers business philosophy underlies everything they do.

"We started 60 because of our love for our city and our passion for food, especially local produce. We have been able to build strong relationships with small local suppliers and share our interests with our customers." 60 offers a traditional, no-fuss approach, classic in style and accommodating to customer's needs. With a large and loyal following, the 60 Supper club has developed, which enables guests to meet the producer whether that be a local food supplier, wine merchant or brewer.

It can be said that the Manning brothers, now with two sister restaurants to 60, are flying the flag high for their own city and for the North West, championing the great quality of what the area has to offer. Long may the flag fly!

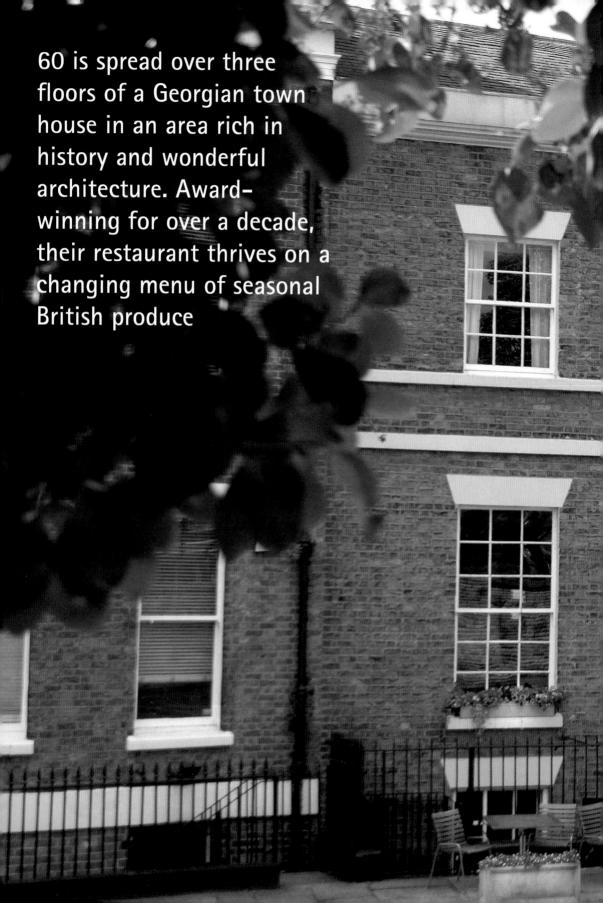

60 is spread over three floors of a Georgian town house in an area rich in history and wonderful architecture. Award-winning for over a decade, their restaurant thrives on a changing menu of seasonal British produce

GOOSNARGH DUCK COTTAGE PIE

SERVES 4

🍷 *2009 Barbera del Montferrato, Tacchino, Piedmont, Italy*

Ingredients

Duck Filling

4 duck legs
50g carrot (diced)
50g celery (diced)
1 apple peeled and (diced)
1 onion (finely diced)
1 tbsp parsley (chopped)
500ml duck fat
150ml brown chicken stock

Mash Topping

1kg potatoes (peeled)
50g butter
1 egg yolk
salt and pepper

Method

For the duck filling

In a large roasting tray, place the duck legs and fat.

Cover with tin foil, place in the oven and cook for approx 6-7 hours on a low heat (110°C) until it is tender and the thigh bone can be removed.

When cooked, remove from the oil, drain and cool.

Remove and discard the skin, flake the leg meat away from the bone, being careful to discard any tendons, leaving shredded duck meat only.

Then roughly chop the shredded duck meat.

In a sauté pan, sweat the carrots, celery and onion in a little butter until translucent.

Add the duck meat, apple, parsley and chicken stock and mix well.

Season to taste.

For the mash topping

Chop the potatoes into equal size pieces and place them in a pan of salted water.

Bring to the boil and simmer for 15-20 minutes until cooked.

Drain and then return to the pan.

Add butter, mash, mix well and season to taste.

When cool, add egg yolk and mix well, this will enrich the potatoes and help glaze the dish when cooked.

Once cool, place the potato in a piping bag and decorate pie.

To assemble

Place the duck filling in an ovenproof dish to either finish off under the grill with the mash topping or place in the oven and cook for 15 -20 minutes on a moderate heat 180°C until hot throughout.

To serve

Assemble as in the picture.

WILD SEA BASS WRAPPED IN POTATO WITH SAMPHIRE, PEAS, BEANS & PANCETTA

SERVES 4

🍷 *2010 Sauvignon de Touraine, Alain Macardet, Loire, France*

Ingredients

4 x 225g sea bass (filleted and skinned)
salt and pepper
4 sprigs of thyme
4kg large potatoes (peeled)
butter (melted)
50g pancetta (sliced)
100g peas (podded)
100g broad beans (blanched and depodded)
150g runner beans (thinly sliced and blanched)
100g samphire
pepper to taste

Method

Preparation

Thinly slice the potato lengthways and lay on a piece of parchment.

Overlap the potato slices like a tiled roof, ensuring that the potato is big enough to wrap around the fish.

Season the sea bass with salt, pepper and thyme.

Place the fish in the centre of the potato slices and, using the parchment, carefully wrap around the fish and seal like a parcel.

Trim off any excess potato to keep the parcel neat.

Brush with melted butter in order to stop the potato discolouring

This can be prepared in advance and refrigerated.

For the peas, beans and pancetta

Gently fry the pancetta in a dry sauté pan until crispy.

Add the peas, beans and samphire.

Warm through and season with pepper.

For the seabass

Slowly warm a non stick pan and place the sea bass in, butter side down, and gently fry for approx 1 minute.

Place in a hot oven at 225°C for approx 5 minutes until golden brown.

Turn fish over and cook for a further 3 minutes until cooked through then rest before serving.

To serve

Serve the fish on the bed of peas, beans, pancetta and samphire.

ELDERFLOWER JELLY & PANNA COTTA WITH CLAREMONT FARM STRAWBERRIES

SERVES 4

🍷 *2007 Muscat de Beaumes de Venise, Domaine de Durban, Rhone, France*

Ingredients

4 glasses

Elderflower Jelly

160ml elderflower cordial
480ml water
1 vanilla pod (deseeded)
3 sheets gelatine (soaked in cold water to soften)

Panna Cotta

360ml double cream
36g caster sugar
66ml full fat milk
1½ sheets of gelatine (soaked in cold water to soften)

Strawberries

1 punnet of strawberries (hulled)
50g icing sugar

Garnish

sprig of mint
mini meringue balls

Method

For the elderflower cordial

In a pan, bring the water to the boil and add the vanilla pod to infuse, then take the pan off the heat.

Add the sheets of gelatine to the pan and stir well until the gelatine dissolves.

Then pass the liquid through a sieve into a large jug to retrieve the vanilla pod and any undissolved gelatine.

Add cordial, mix and place in the fridge for 5 minutes.

Pour into glasses or moulds and leave to set in fridge.

For the panna cotta

Bring the milk to the boil in a pan, together with the caster sugar. Take off the heat and add the gelatine. Stir gently to dissolve and pass through a sieve.

Add to the cream, mix well and allow to cool. Pour onto set jelly when cool enough not to melt the jelly. Then place back in fridge and chill.

When set it is ready to dress and serve.

For the strawberries

In a blender, blitz ¼ of the punnet of strawberries with the icing sugar and pass through a sieve to make the coulis.

Chop the rest of the strawberries and mix with the coulis.

Place on top of the panna cotta.

To serve

Garnish with a sprig of mint and mini meringue balls.

030
THE BAY HORSE INN

Bay Horse Lane, Bay Horse, Ellel, Lancaster LA2 OHR

01524 791 204
www.bayhorseinn.com

The Bay Horse is conveniently located only minutes from the motorway, down a country lane off the A6. Sitting on the edge of the Trough of Bowland, from the dining room and the back garden of the pub there are views over picturesque Lancashire farmland. The coast can be reached in less than 20 minutes and the Lake District is less than an hour away.

Inside the pub, you'll find open fires, a warm welcome, and friendly staff waiting to meet your needs. The ambience is relaxed and informal, although you won't feel out of place in your Sunday best, should you choose to dress up. The bar area also provides room for dining, with the dining room itself having a slightly more formal feel. Tables in both areas are equally popular and are often chosen to reflect the occasion and individual preference. From the dining room, you can access the landscaped gardens, which provide plenty of tables for those days when the sun shines.

Craig aims to ensure that the food is of the best quality, without being pretentious or fussy. Lancashire favourites are served alongside a selection of more innovative dishes and clean flavours are key. Craig has been the chef at the pub for nearly twenty years and his skill and style have been honed over that time. Located across the road from the pub, in a converted grain barn you will find the 'Corn Store', which provides luxury accommodation with two en-suite rooms. Each room is individually designed with comfortable beds and lovely en-suite bathrooms. Both rooms are equipped with flat screen TV's, iPod docks and wi-fi.

The ambience is relaxed and informal, although you won't feel out of place in your Sunday best, should you choose to dress up

MELON, CURED HAM, CREAMED GOAT'S CHEESE, PEAS & RAPESEED OIL

SERVES 4

 *Grand Ardechè Chardonnay*

Method

For the creamed goat's cheese

Cream the goat's cheese together with the double cream and season to taste.

To serve

Plate up three slices of melon with three spoons of the creamed goat's cheese. Then arrange three slices of cured ham on top of the cheese with some peas, red vein sorrel and a little of the rapeseed oil poured around and over to finish.

Ingredients

2 Ogen melon (skinned, seeded and sliced)
12 slices of cured ham (local or Parma)
150g of peas
1 small punnet red vein sorrel
virgin rapeseed oil

Creamed Goat's Cheese

250g goat's cheese
175ml double cream
salt and white pepper

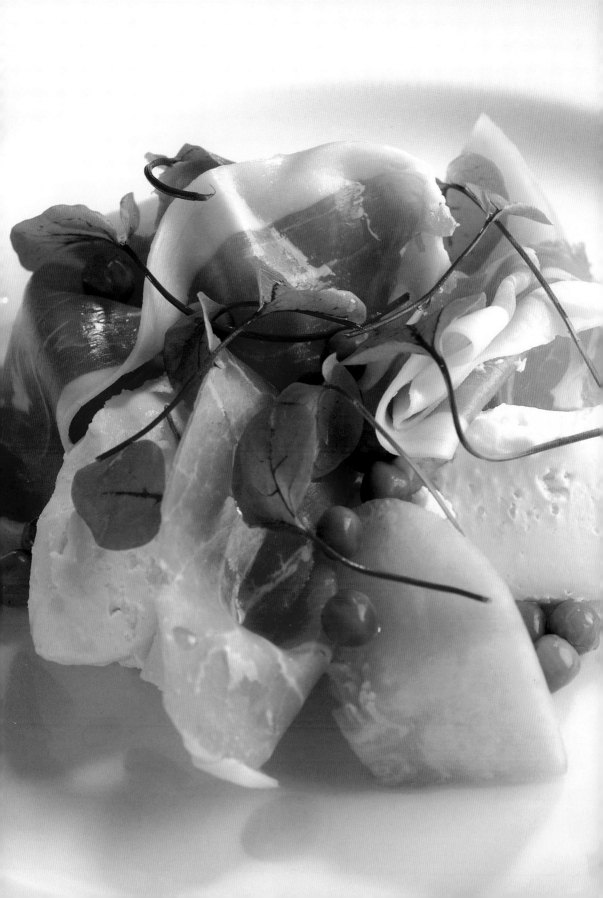

HALIBUT WITH CRAB POTATOES & ASPARAGUS

SERVES 4

 Groote Post Chenin Blanc

Ingredients

4 x 250g halibut fillets
12 spears asparagus
200g cherry plum tomatoes (washed and halved)

Crab Potatoes

800g new potatoes or Jersey Royals (cooked and halved)
200g cooked white and brown crab meat
a handful of chives (chopped)

Dressing

handful of garden herbs (chervil and flat parsley are best)
virgin olive oil
pinch of salt

Garnish

chervil (picked and washed)
rocket cress (washed)
broad beans (blanched for 2 minutes and peeled)
herb oil

Method

For the asparagus

Break or cut off the bottom third of the asparagus spears, blanch for 2 minutes in boiling, salted water with a little sugar. Plunge into ice water to stop further cooking and set aside.

For the crab potatoes

Mix the cooked potatoes with the crab meat and the chopped chives and season to taste. Keep warm until needed.

For the dressing

Whizz up a handful of washed garden herbs in a food processor with some virgin olive oil and a pinch of salt.

For the halibut

Lightly fry the halibut fillet in a little olive oil using a non stick frying pan, skin-side down for a minute or so. Then roast in the oven (200°C), skin-side down, for 6 minutes. Take out of the oven, turn it over and allow to rest in the pan for a couple of minutes so that the halibut is around 57°C in the middle.

To serve

Warm the asparagus under a hot grill with a little butter. Arrange some of the crab potatoes on warm plates with 3 asparagus spears and cherry tomatoes and then place the halibut fillets on top. Garnish with the picked chervil, rocket cress and the broad beans then pour a little of the herb oil around and over.

SET VANILLA YOGHURT WITH BOOZY STRAWBERRIES, SHORTBREAD AND BLACK PEPPER CARAMEL

SERVES 4

 Tokaji 3 Puttonyos

Ingredients

Strawberries
2 large punnets of strawberries
150ml strawberry liqueur

Yoghurt
200g double cream
640g sweet plain yoghurt
5 gelatine leaves (soaked in cold water)
honey (2 dessert spoons)
vanilla pod (with the seeds scraped out)

Strawberry Sauce
icing sugar
left over strawberries

Caramel
100g caster sugar
black pepper
mint leaves (washed and picked)
shortbread (small packet)

Method

For the strawberries

Marinate a punnet and a half of the strawberries overnight in the strawberry liqueur.

For the yoghurt

Warm the cream in a saucepan and add the soaked gelatine leaves, honey and the vanilla seeds. Next, warm the yoghurt in a microwave on a medium setting to around 50°C and then whisk in the cream mixture. Pass the mixture through a fine sieve into some ramekins and set overnight in the fridge.

For the strawberry sauce

Whizz up the remaining strawberries in a food processor with a little icing sugar to taste until smooth.

For the caramel

In a sugar pan, place the caster sugar and a drop of water and slowly bring to the boil until a blonde caramel forms (don't stir the caramel). Take off the heat and cool a little, then grind in a couple of turns of black pepper to taste and stir it in.

To serve

De-mould the yoghurts and place them on the plates. Next, arrange some of the marinated strawberries on the plates with some strawberry sauce, a few dots of caramel, mint leaves and some crumbled shortbread. Then serve.

040
THE BUBBLE ROOM

1 Woolton Street, Liverpool L25 5NH

0151 909 4909
www.thebubbleroom.co.uk

The Bubble Room is one of Liverpool's newest restaurants and is located in Woolton Village, south of Liverpool City Centre and situated next door to the restored, famous Elephant Pub, which is also operated by the same owners; a great excuse for staying local.

Offering well cooked and inspired meals, Head Chef James Connolly and his brother and Sous Chef John are firm believers in using seasonal products sourcing only the best local produce available to create exciting twists on classic dishes served in a relaxed but professional manner. Meals are complemented with the finest wines, champagnes and premium spirits, with a cocktail list the envy of many city centre bars.

The Bubble Room is best described as shabby chic, with a big splash of distorted glamour. Open for breakfast, brunch, lunch and dinner, The Bubble Room can meet your needs any time of the day, a comfortable and relaxed place to be and be seen.

So that's it; The Bubble Room, unique, sophisticated with comfortable interiors, great freshly cooked locally sourced food, combined with a friendly service to match our cocktails, wine and fizz.

Offering well cooked and inspired meals, Head Chef James Connolly and his brother and Sous Chef John are firm believers in using seasonal products sourcing only the best local produce available to create exciting twists on classic dishes served in a relaxed but professional manner.

PAN FRIED HAND DIVED SCALLOPS, WITH PANCETTA, BLACK PUDDING, PEA AND RED PEPPER PUREE

SERVES 4

🍷 *Australian Chardonnay*

Ingredients

16 scallops
(Bought in their shell if possible as it enhances the flavours)

Pea Puree

1 kg frozen peas
1 large onion
4 heads garlic
1 litre vegetable stock
1 potato

Red Pepper Puree

4 red peppers

70g smoked bacon
(Other types of bacon can be used; pancetta or even chorizo sausage)

70g black pudding
(We use Jack Wood butchers in Failsworth, Manchester for both the black pudding and smoked bacon)

Method

For the scallops

Season the scallops with salt and a little mild curry powder, and lightly massage a little olive oil into each one. Heat up a non-stick frying pan. Once the pan is very hot, add a small amount of oil. Place the scallops flat into the pan, on the largest side. This will also be the side you serve them on. After about 90 seconds you should notice that the scallops have started to colour, gently turn them at this point and add a small knob of butter, a squeeze of lemon juice and a little sea salt. Allow around 30 seconds to cook then remove from the pan.

For the pea puree

Finely dice the onion, garlic and potato. Sauté the onion, garlic and potato in a stock pan. Do not colour. Once softened, add the vegetable stock. Bring the stock to the boil and add the peas, then leave to boil for 2 minutes. Place the mix into a blender or liquidiser and blitz to a puree, then season. Pass the mix though a fine sieve into a mixing bowl that is on top of an ice bath, this will retain the colour of the puree. Place into a tub, label, and keep in the fridge until needed. Puree should last for 3 days.

For the red pepper puree

Firstly, roast the peppers by placing them in a roasting tray and baking them at 200°C until the peppers' skins start to blister. Once the skin has blistered, remove from the tray and place in a deep bowl and cover with clingfilm. Leave for 20 minutes to steam, which will make the blistered skin easier to remove. Now remove the skin and dice the peppers' flesh. Place in a saucepan and slow-cook the peppers until they are soft enough to be blended into a puree. Remove from the blender and store in a tub until needed. Puree should last for 3 days.

For the smoked bacon

Dice into nice sized cubes and fry in a frying pan until crisp and golden.

For the black pudding

Simply grill until cooked.

To serve

To dress the plate and serve is easy and quick. Firstly, swipe a teaspoon of the warm pea puree and a teaspoon of the red pepper puree on to the plate, then arrange the smoked bacon, black pudding and scallops and finally finish the dish with a little drizzle of lemon juice and chopped chive.

SWEET AND SOUR SEA BASS WITH PINEAPPLE, CRAB AND BABY CARROTS

SERVES 4

 *Shiraz Tempranillo Rose*

Ingredients

Sea Bass

6 sea bass fillets (1½ fillets per person)

Pineapple Fondant

1 pineapple
2 measures of Malibu
100g brown sugar
1 star anise (crushed to a dust)
150g butter

Pineapple Relish

300g excess pineapple
2 chillies (diced)
100ml white wine vinegar
150g caster sugar
200g crab meat

Sweet and Sour Glaze

red wine vinegar
brown sugar
ketchup
pineapple juice
fish stock
16 baby carrots

Method

For the pineapple fondant

Firstly, and with a sharp knife, remove the top and head of the pineapple then slice off the skin and throw it away. Find the core and cut the pineapple away from it. Using a small cutter, cut out some fondants - you should easily get 8 good size fondants from a pineapple. Don't throw any of the excess pineapple away, keep it for the relish. Heat up a frying pan and remember, be careful when working with hot sugar! Place the brown sugar in the pan with the butter then add the pineapple fondants, the star anise and the Malibu. Gently rotate the pan, causing the ingredients to make a rich caramel sauce. Let the pineapple cook for a few minutes in the sauce. Once the fondant is covered in a nice glaze remove it from the pan.

For the pineapple relish

Add the vinegar and the sugar to a medium size pan, and start to gently heat them. Once hot, add the chilli and pineapple. Now leave this to cook for around 15 minutes on a medium heat, you should notice that the sugar has started to caramelise and the pineapple has broken down to resemble a chutney or relish. At this point remove the pan from the heat, leave to cool then add the crabmeat.

For the sweet and sour glaze

Simply peel the carrots and blanch them in hot, salted water for a few minutes. You want the carrots to have a slight bite to them. Remove from the hot water and place into iced water, this will stop the cooking process and also retain the colour. Place in a tub till later.

For the seabass

Firstly season the fish lightly with salt and cracked black pepper, then heat up a non stick frying pan. Once the pan is hot, add a little oil and a pinch of salt. The salt will help stop the fish sticking to the pan. Now add the fish to the pan, skin side down, and leave for around 2 minutes. Do not turn it. After 2 minutes you should notice changes in the fish colour, now turn the fish over. Drizzle in some of the sweet and sour glaze. This should slightly bubble and spit out of the pan so be careful. Now gently rotate the fish and the sauce around the pan for around one minute, this will glaze the fish and finish cooking it. At this point you can add the carrots. Place on a low heat and dress the plate.

To serve

Firstly, take a little of the excess sauce from the pan and drizzle it on the plate. Then take some of the warm pineapple and crab relish and place in the centre of the plate. Add a warm pineapple fondant at one end of the plate and the baby carrots at the other. Gently add the sea bass on the relish. And that's it, enjoy!

TIRAMISU

SERVES 4

The Bubble Room's Godfather cocktail

Ingredients

Chocolate Mousse

150g dark chocolate
250ml cream
2 egg yolks
25g caster sugar
2 egg whites

Cake Base

125g dark chocolate
120g unsalted butter
100g caster sugar
2 whole eggs
65g plain flour

Espresso Mousse

400ml whipping cream
1 shot of espresso
1 measure of amaretto
40g icing sugar

Temper Chocolate Disc

100g dark chocolate
1 temperature probe

Chocolate Sauce

125g dark chocolate
30g cream

Method

For the chocolate mousse

Firstly, whip the cream and egg whites to soft peaks, and leave them in a cool place. Melt the chocolate over a bain marie, and once melted, leave in a warm area so it stays melted.

To make the sabayon, whisk the yolks and sugar over a bain marie. Once the yolks are glossy remove them from the heat. Now add the chocolate, this will form a thick mix. Add the whipped cream and egg whites to the mix to form a soft mousse. Place in the fridge and leave to set for a few hours.

For the cake base

Firstly pre-heat the oven to 180°C and line a flat baking tray with greaseproof paper. Melt the chocolate in a heatproof bowl over some gently simmering water and remove when soft. Beat together the butter and sugar. Once beaten together, add the eggs one at a time and beat again. Now mix in the chocolate. Using a large spoon or spatula slowly add the flour. By using a spoon you can retain the air in the mix to make it softer. Pour the mix on to a baking tray and spread thinly to about half a centimetre. Bake for 5 minutes. Remove from the oven and leave to cool.

For the espresso mousse

Add the espresso and amaretto together and leave to cool. Then whip the cream to a soft peak, add the cold espresso mix and sweeten with the sugar.

For the temper chocolate disc

Firstly, line a flat tray with greaseproof paper. Heat the chocolate in a heatproof bowl over gently simmering water. You need to take the chocolate to the exact temperature to get the correct texture and shine. The first temperature is 48°C. Once at that temperature leave it to cool to 28°C then reheat to 35°C. Pour and spread thinly on the greaseproof paper and leave to cool.

For the chocolate sauce

Melt the two items in a heatproof bowl over gently simmering water. Once mixed together it's complete. Keep warm till needed.

To serve

You will need 4 round cake cutters, around 10cm wide, and 2 piping bags. Place the chocolate mousse in to one of the piping bags and the espresso mousse into the other. Cut out 4 discs of the tempered chocolate and leave to one side, then cut 4 cake bases. Place one cake base on to the plate and place the cake cutter around the base, pipe in the chocolate mousse around the edge of the ring, then pipe the espresso mousse inside the chocolate mousse. Remove the cake cutter and place the temper chocolate ring on top of the tiramisu and pour the chocolate sauce on top and serve.

050
THE DUKE OF YORK

Brow Top, Grindleton, Near Clitheroe, Lancashire BB7 4QR

01200 441 266
www.dukeofyorkgrindleton.com

Following a thorough but sympathetic refurbishment of the kitchen, bar and dining room in late 2007, Michael Heathcote has firmly established The Duke of York as one of the Ribble Valley's leading pub/restaurants, attracting scores of guests from far and wide who are keen to sample the restaurant which is commonly known amongst regulars as "Lancashire's best-kept culinary secret". The Duke of York serves classic British food with a modern and unique twist, showcasing not only the great skill of the kitchen team, but also their sense of humour. Menus can change twice daily as Michael, alongside head chef Robert Geldeard, makes the most of the amazing local produce the Ribble Valley has to offer. Dishes aren't overly complicated, which allows the fantastic, seasonal produce to shine through. With a crackling log fire, a warm welcome awaits guests during the colder months, whilst in the summer a beautiful garden area offers al-fresco dining. Michael Heathcote is a proud Lancastrian born and raised in Pleasington, and his passion for food stems from an early age when he helped his grandparents bake biscuits for their business in Blackburn. Michael trained in several establishments across England and Wales before setting off to gain experience in top restaurants in Australia, Canada and the USA. On his return, he became head chef at Borrowdale Gates Country House Hotel in Cumbria, leading the kitchen for 8 years and achieving 2AA rosettes and entries in the Good Food Guide every year, before returning to the Ribble Valley to open the Duke of York.

UKE OF YORK

With a crackling log fire, a warm welcome awaits guests during the colder months, whilst in the summer a beautiful garden area offers al-fresco dining

BOUILLABAISSE

SERVES 6

🍷 *Sancerre Rose 2010, Domaine Hubert Brochard, Loire Valley*

Ingredients

Fish

6 King scallops
12 King prawn tails
36 Shetland mussels
1 monkfish tail (cut into 6 medallions)
samphire

Bisque

1 each of onion, leek, fennel bulb, carrot, head of garlic
2 sticks of celery
2 red peppers
200g coriander seeds
5 star anise
5 cardamom pods
200g fennel seeds
4 kaffir lime leaves
100g fresh ginger
2 red chillies
2 stalks of lemongrass
good splash of brandy (approx 100ml)
3 tbsp tomato puree
1 kg crab bones
enough water to cover

Method

For the bisque

Roast the crab bones in an oven for 15 minutes at 180°C. Sweat off the vegetables until softened, then add the crab bones as well as the spices and aromatics. Add brandy, flame and reduce, then add the tomato puree and enough water to cover. Simmer until it is reduced by half then pass through a colander, and then again through muslin cloth. Season to taste with salt and lemon.

For the fish

Sear the scallops and monkfish in a hot pan for no more than 30 seconds per side and finish with butter.

Steam the mussels in white wine for 1-2 minutes until open.

Cook the king prawns and samphire in the hot bisque for 1 minute.

Place the shellfish in a bowl and pour in bisque.

To serve

Assemble as in the picture.

ASSIETTE OF RABBIT

SERVES 2

 Galpin Peak Pinot Noir 2009, Bouchard Finlayson, Walker Bay, South Africa

Ingredients

1 whole rabbit (butchered into loin, rack & legs)

Ballontine

100g chicken breast (diced)
250ml double cream
Tarragon
4 sheets air dried ham

Rilette

duck fat (enough to cover the legs)
3 garlic cloves (minced)
1 tbsp parsley (chopped)
2 tbsp sherry vinegar

Garnish

Chantenay carrots
girolle mushrooms
broad beans

Method

For the rabbit

Take the cuts of rabbit, season and roast the rack in a hot pan for 1-2 minutes until pink. Finish with butter.

Wrap the loin in clingfilm and cook for 10 minutes in 64°C water, then finish in a hot pan with a little butter.

For the ballontine

Blitz the chicken until smooth, slowly adding the cream, and season with salt and tarragon.

Lay out a sheet of clingfilm on a bench and then lay out two sheets of air dried ham. On top of this, spread a layer of chicken mousse approximately ½ cm thick.

Place the rabbit loin in the centre and tightly roll it into a barrel shape.

Cook the ballontine in 70°C water for 12 minutes.

For the rilette

Cover the rabbit legs in duck fat and confit for 3 hours at 150°C. Allow to cool.

Once cool, strip the meat from the bone and pulse in a blender with other ingredients.

Then tightly roll in clingfilm and chill.

Warm the rilette in a hot oven for 2-3 minutes when ready to serve

For the vegetables

Blanch the broad beans in salted water for 1 minute then peel them.

Blanch the carrots for two minutes in salted water.

Sautee the mushrooms in butter.

To serve

Assemble as in picture, and garnish with broad beans, carrots and wild mushrooms.

CRÈME BRULÉE WITH PIMMS NO. 1 SORBET AND MINT JELLY

SERVES 6-8

🍷 *Tokaji 5 Puttonyos 2003, Chateau Dereszla, Hungary*

Ingredients

Crème Brulée

150g caster sugar
8 egg yolks
250ml whole milk
750ml double cream
1 vanilla pod (split)

Pimms No. 1 Sorbet

200g sugar
200ml Pimms No. 1
200ml soda water
200ml water
50ml orange juice
juice of ½ a lemon

Mint Jelly

250g sugar
250ml water
5 gelatine leaves
10 sprigs fresh mint

Caramel Discs

200ml liquid glucose
50ml water
200g sugar

Method

For the crème brulée

Bring the milk, cream and split vanilla pod to the boil. Separately beat the egg yolk and sugar together in a mixing bowl. Pour ⅓ of the milk and cream mix onto the egg mixture and continue beating. Add the mix back into the pan and cook on a low heat whilst continually stirring until the mixture has reached 85°C. Pour into moulds and refrigerate.

For the pimms No. 1 sorbet

Dissolve the sugar in the water and boil rapidly for 5-6 minutes before adding all the other ingredients. Then churn and freeze.

For the mint jelly

Add sugar and water to a heavy-based pan. Slowly bring it to the boil until the sugar has completely dissolved. Then add mint leaves and leave to infuse for 30 minutes. Pass the liquid through a fine sieve, then add gelatine leaves to the liquid and allow it to dissolve. Once dissolved, pour the mixture into a chilled tray and leave to set.

For the caramel discs

Heat all the ingredients together until the sugar has completely dissolved, and then boil rapidly until golden caramel in colour. Carefully remove from the heat and pour onto a sheet of baking parchment, then leave for 15 minutes until completely cool and brittle. Blitz to a powder. Spread out a thin layer of the powder (approx 2mm thick) in a circle between 2 sheets of baking parchment, then bake in a hot oven until the powder has melted and leave to cool.

To serve

Place a quenelle of Pimms sorbet on top of the set crème brulée. Scatter some pieces of mint jelly around the sorbet. Sit a caramel disc on top of the glass and then gently soften the edges so it sticks to the glass rim.

Chef's tip

If you do not have an ice cream machine then freeze the sorbet immediately and blitz in a food processor.

060
THE FENCE GATE AT FENCE

Wheatley Lane Road, Fence, Nr Burnley, Lancashire BB12 9EE

01282 618 101
www.fencegate.co.uk

The Fence Gate was purchased in 1982 by master butcher and entrepreneur Kevin Berkins, who has been at the helm for what is now looming 30 years. Previously a small restaurant seen as having potential, Fence Gate was originally a 17th Century home to local squires. With vigour it was extensively modernised and turned into an Inn with a charming public bar and two function rooms which accommodate a total of 400 guests. The Topiary Brasserie was added in 1997 with a capacity of over 100.

Today the Topiary Brasserie, with Spencer Burge as Head Chef, is renowned for its uncompromising standards of food and service.

Kevin and Spencer, being passionate about fresh food, insist on using as much local produce as possible. They are both keen supporters of the "Dug this Morning" campaign, and so use fresh vegetables from local farmers.

Fence Gate has been rewarded for their efforts. Their menus have tickled the taste buds of local people as well as food critics from afar. Recognition for this has come from Michelin among many others.

In 2007 Kevin snatched 'The Oscars' of the pub industry at the Publican Awards, and was awarded the accolade of 'Free House of the Year 2007'. One of Kevin's highlights has to be being crowned BPEX Supreme Sausage Champion 2010 at the Butchers Hall, Smithsfield. This triggered the opening of 'Berkins Deli' at their sister site, The Eagle at Barrow, Nr. Clitheroe. Fence Gate's countless awards include 'Best Sunday Lunch' Observer Awards, 'Best Dessert Pub of the Year', 'Local Food Champion of the Year', 'Lancashire Restaurant of the Year', 'Wine List of the Year', the

awards are endless. The Deli is now the home of the Champion Sausage which, along with its 35 day dry aging refrigerator cabinets housing Rib Eye and Sirloin Steaks, is a welcome addition. There is also a selection of dry cure bacon and home cured salmon, smoked in their on-site smoke house.

What you can say about the team at Fence Gate is, that they are all very passionate about food.

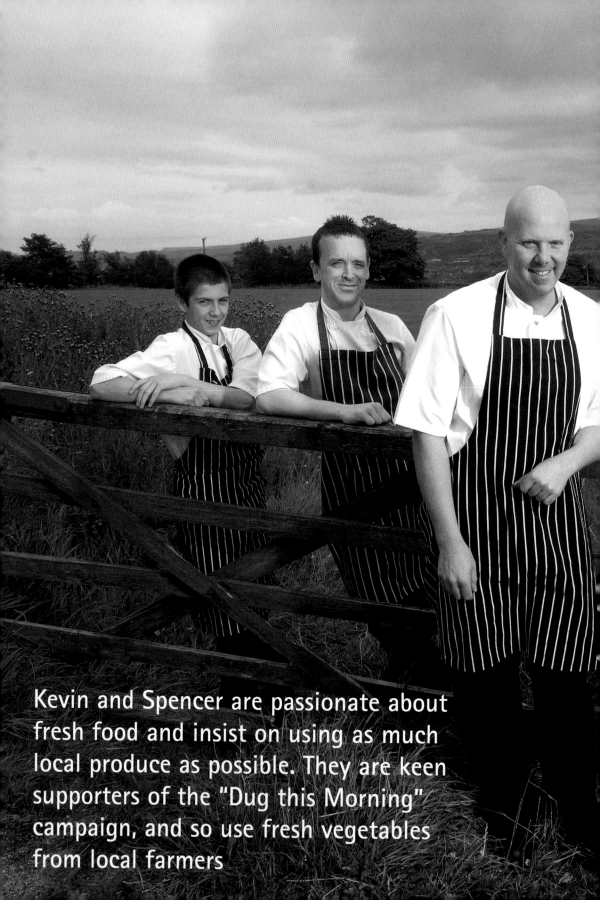

Kevin and Spencer are passionate about fresh food and insist on using as much local produce as possible. They are keen supporters of the "Dug this Morning" campaign, and so use fresh vegetables from local farmers

HAM HOCK AND TARRAGON TERRINE, HOME SMOKED PANCETTA, BLACK PUDDING BON BONS, PEA AND WHITE TRUFFLE VELOUTE

SERVES 12

🍷 *Joseph Mellot 2008 Pouilly-Fumé Cuveé Troncsec, France*

Ingredients

Ham Hock Terrine

1.5kg ham hock
1 bouquet garni
(2 bay leaves, sprig thyme, 2 sprigs parsley)
mirepoix of vegetables (2 carrots, 2 onions, 1 stick celery)
80g fresh tarragon
salt and pepper
3 litres water

Black Pudding Bon Bons

240g black pudding
4 eggs
50g flour
50g fine breadcrumbs

Pea and Ham Veloute

1 litre of ham stock
800g garden peas (frozen)
250g butter (diced)
6 sprigs of mint
60g smoked pancetta

Method

For the ham hock terrine

Bring the ham hocks to a rolling boil for 1 minute and skim off any impurities that float to the surface. Then reduce to a simmer and add the bouquet garni, mirepoix and tarragon stalks (keeping tarragon leaves).

Simmer for 6 hours until meat starts to fall off the bones, then pick off the meat, discarding any fat or bone.

Chop the tarragon leaves and add them to the meat, then season with the salt and pepper. Take some of the cooking liquid and strain it. Reduce it by half and pour onto the mixture.

Line a 23cm x 9cm x 8cm mould and press the mixture to form a terrine.

For the black pudding bon bons

Mould the black pudding into small balls. Prepare them for frying by giving them a light dusting of flour then egg wash and finally by dipping them into the breadcrumbs.

Deep fry until golden brown and drain them of excess oil on absorbent paper.

For the pea and ham veloute

Bring the ham stock to the boil.

Place the thawed garden peas into a food processor and add the diced butter and mint.

Switch the food processor on and pour on the boiling stock until a smooth bright green consistency is achieved. Season.

Dice pancetta very finely and fry until crispy.

To serve

Plate as seen in picture.

PAN SEARED WILD SEABASS WITH MORECAMBE BAY SHRIMP, CRAB AND CHILLI RAVIOLI, ORIENTAL VEGETABLES AND WASABI HOLLANDAISE

SERVES 5

 La Versa 2008 Pinot Noir Blanc, Italy

Ingredients

Seabass

5 x 180g wild seabass fillet
50g butter
20ml oil
salt and pepper

Shrimp, Crab and Chilli Ravioli

100g Morecambe Bay shrimp
50g white crab meat
20g coriander (chopped)
2 red chilli (finely diced)
½ tsp dried ginger
100g brie cheese
salt and pepper
300g fresh pasta dough

Wasabi Hollandaise (makes 200ml)

3 tbsp of white wine vinegar reduction
2 egg yolks
150ml clarified butter
salt and pepper
few drops of lemon juice
1 tbsp of parsley (chopped)
wasabi paste

Oriental Vegetables

2 pak choi
½ leek
1 carrot
100g beansprout
60g fresh ginger
1 tbsp coriander (chopped)
1 red pepper
1 yellow pepper
1 tsp garlic puree

Method

For the seabass

Season the fish with salt and pepper then slash the skin. Heat a heavy-based frying pan and add oil. Once hot, fry the fish skin-side down until the skin is crisp and golden. The fish will be almost cooked through. Turn over, add butter, and cook for another minute, spooning the foamed butter over the fish. Remove and serve.

For the shrimp, crab and chilli ravioli

To make the filling for the ravioli place all of the ingredients except the shrimp into a container and kneed them together. When softened, add the shrimp and form the mixture into 50g balls.

Roll out the Pasta dough to a thickness of 2mm. Cut out with a 3" round cutter and brush with a little water around the edge. Place the shrimp balls in the centre and place a slightly bigger round of dough on top. Gently push around the filling to seal the edges.

Blanch in boiling, salted water for 3-4 minutes until al dente.

For the wasabi hollandaise

Put the vinegar reduction into a stainless steel bowl and set over a pan of simmering water. The base of the bowl should not come into contact with the water.

Add the egg yolks and whisk together until the mixture is thick, pale and creamy. Slowly trickle in the clarified butter, whisking continuously until the sauce is thick and shiny. Remove from the heat then season and add the lemon juice, parsley and wasabi paste to taste.

For the oriental vegetables

Wok-fry the vegetables, adding grated ginger and garlic puree. Finish with chopped coriander.

To serve

Assemble as in the picture.

STRAWBERRY TEXTURES & CREAM

SERVES 6

 *Louis Roederer Rich Sec Carte Blanche N.V,
France*

Ingredients

Jelly

100g caster sugar
300ml water
500g strawberries (chilled)
6g powdered gelatine

Honeycomb

625g caster sugar
125ml honey
300g glucose
300ml water
35g bicarbonate of soda

Meringue

3 egg whites
100g caster sugar
100g icing sugar

Strawberry Coulis

250g strawberries (hulled)
2 tsp brown sugar
1 vanilla pod
3 tbsp Grand Marnier or Kirsch

Crème Patissiere

150ml milk
20ml cream
1 vanilla pod
3 egg yolks
50g caster sugar
8g cornflour
10g plain flour

Ice Cream (optional accompaniment)

250g strawberries
90g caster sugar
250ml double cream
2 vanilla pods
5 egg yolks
1 tbsp lemon juice

Method

For the jelly

Place the sugar and water in a pan and bring to the boil for 5 minutes, then leave to cool. Puree the strawberries and pour the sugar syrup into the puree. Once cool, pass through a sieve. Place a ¼ cup of cold water into a small dish, leave for 5 minutes. Heat 100ml of the strawberry mix, then place gelatine into the water and gently simmer to dissolve. Mix the lukewarm liquid with the remaining strawberry puree and leave to set.

For the honeycomb

Boil the sugar, honey, glucose and water until it turns light caramel. While this is happening, greaseproof a large tray. Add bicarbonate of soda to the caramel and whisk quickly. Beware that it doubles in size, so make sure the pan is big enough. Pour the caramel onto the greaseproof tray and allow to cool.

For the meringue

Put the egg whites and a few tablespoons of caster sugar into a clean mixer. Whisk at a low speed, then increase the speed to high until the mixture thickens to a smooth, soft, glossy peak. Sift the remaining caster sugar until it forms firm peaks, then briefly whisk in icing sugar. Pipe into shape and leave overnight at 60°C until crisp.

For the strawberry coulis

Heat the vanilla, sugar and strawberries until the sugar dissolves then add Grand Marnier or Kirsch and heat for another 30 seconds. Leave to cool. Puree and pass through a sieve.

For the crème patissiere

Put the milk, cream and vanilla pod in a pan and bring to the boil. Whisk egg yolks and sugar until it reaches the ribbon stage, then fold in the cornflour and sifted flour. Pour a third of the liquid onto the egg mixture and whisk to combine. Pour back into the saucepan and cook on a moderate heat until it thickens to a glossy smooth paste. Stand in a bowl of iced water. Remove vanilla pod and whisk vigorously to beat out any lumps.

For the ice cream

Bring the milk and cream nearly to the boil along with the vanilla pods, then leave to allow the flavour to infuse. Whisk the egg yolks and sugar until pale and thick. Remove the vanilla pods and pour the warm liquid onto the egg mixture and whisk. Put back onto the heat and stir until thickened, then put into a cool bowl. Puree the strawberries and pass through a sieve, then fold the strawberry puree into the cooled mix and place into an ice cream machine until churned.

To serve

Assemble as in the picture.

070
FRAICHE

11 Rose Mount, Oxton, Wirral CH43 5SG

0151 652 2914
www.restaurantfraiche.com

Small but beautiful; A serene restaurant hidden away in Oxton, a small conservation village situated on the Wirral, Fraiche is a 16 cover venue which has lead the pack in Merseyside since opening in 2004 and being the first Michelin starred restaurant in the county, along with other plaudits. Fraiche is all about Marc Wilkinson and his drive to push tastes, textures and temperatures in new directions for his guests to savour. Eating at Fraiche is about living Marc's passion for the elegant, calming décor based on the sea shore, with soft colours designed and refurbished by the chef with little outside help. Enriched by stunning commissioned glass art created by local Liverpool artist Jenny Barker, all set the scene for a unique dining experience which Wilkinson has evolved on a firm foundation of French classical cuisine, leading onto his modern approach of clean flavour hits throughout a meal. Techniques and modern tools bring out true flavours and purity in the dishes. To keep flavours clean Marc uses very little cream and butter and barely any wine, utilising fruit juices in their place, although the wine list itself is also compiled with passion, as it holds over 300 wines with special mention to half bottles and an impressive sherry listing. It is award-winning in its own right.

The obsession doesn't stop there; even the music is chosen to complement the time of the evening and the tempo is considered. Plates and glassware, bespoke in construction, finish off the package.

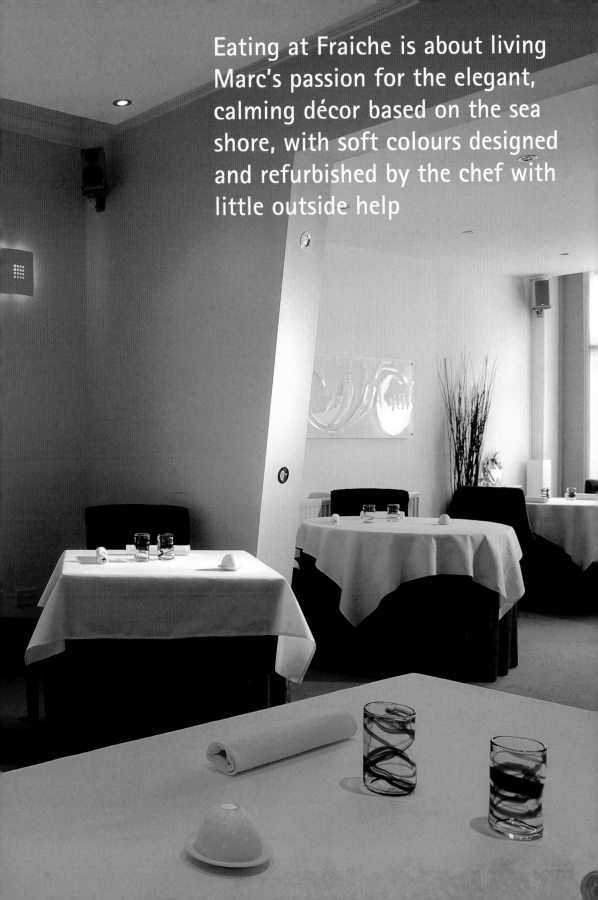

Eating at Fraiche is about living Marc's passion for the elegant, calming décor based on the sea shore, with soft colours designed and refurbished by the chef with little outside help

ROASTED BUTTERNUT SQUASH, PARMESAN ICE CREAM AND TEXTURES OF WOODLAND MUSHROOM

SERVES 4

 Pinot Grigio from Veneto

Ingredients

Truffle Dressing

micro salads
brioche croutons
Sosa forest aroma
chicken wing based jus

Butternut Squash

1 butternut squash
3 to 4 sage leaves
55g unsalted butter
2 tbsp orange juice
salt and white pepper

Parmesan Ice-Cream

150g parmesan (finely grated)
50g glucose
500ml milk
30g dextrose
15g pro crema (Sosa)

Mushroom Textures

chestnut mushrooms (raw, sliced on a mandolin)
shimeji mushrooms
cep mushrooms (fresh or frozen but not dried)
winter black truffle
shitake mushrooms

Method

For the butternut squash

At the restaurant we peel and dice the squash into squares, place into a sous vide bag with the rest of the ingredients and vacuum pack it. It is then cooked for 15 - 20 minutes at 85°C and refreshed in iced water. It is then put aside until it is needed.

For the parmesan ice-cream

Heat the milk with the glucose and dextrose and pour over the cheese and pro crema. Blend well, pass through a muslin cloth and chill before freezing in a paco beaker to set up ready. We make this the day before to ensure the mix is completely solid.

For the mushroom textures

The cep mushroom element is confit in olive oil, thyme with garlic and tomatoes, and also a touch of lemon juice.

The shimeji are trimmed and lightly pickled. We use rice wine vinegar at Fraiche.

The shitake are prepared for sauté and a few chestnut mushrooms are sliced in half or quarters depending on size.

To finish

Sauté the mushrooms in a hot pan with olive oil and butter. As they cook, add the butternut dice and place in the oven to roast. After 4 to 5 minutes take out of the oven, then add a little jus to glaze the mix and adjust the seasoning (we use smoked salt for this part).

To serve

Build the plate with the raw mushrooms, brioche croutons and the pickled mushrooms. The confit ceps are now added to the butternut mix to warm through and placed around the plate.

Quenelle the ice cream, place in the centre of the plate and top with truffle and finish with truffle dressing. Use the aroma on the dish at the last second using an aroma gun.

Chef's tip

You can also create a snow effect with the ice cream mix as the cheese helps to set the mix quite hard, we use it on another dish as a powder.

ROASTED QUAIL, BEETROOT AND TRUFFLED BARLEY

SERVES 4

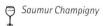 *Saumur Champigny*

Ingredients

Quails
4 whole quails
fresh thyme
50ml olive oil
25g butter

Barley
200g barley (washed)
1 tbsp truffle (chopped)
50g chicken stock (or quail if possible)
20g butter (unsalted)
lemon juice to taste

Beetroots
4 large organic beetroots
course salt
25ml elderflower cordial
25ml water
15g butter
tsp of lemon juice

Sauce
300ml of brown chicken stock (or quail if possible)
100ml Madeira
100ml port
sprig of fresh thyme
1 bay leaf
butter (diced)

Method

For the beetroots

Sit the unpeeled beetroots on a generous bed of salt and bake in the oven at 180°C until soft to the touch.

Allow to cool, then remove the top and bottom. Using an apple corer, take out cylinders of beetroot flesh. Warm these through in the elderflower cordial diluted with water, butter and lemon juice.

For the quails

To season the birds, place thyme and butter into the cavities. Then heat a pan with a little olive oil and lay the quail into the hot pan and allow it to colour on both sides for a couple of minutes. Once they are golden, place the pan in a preheated oven at 180°C for 6 - 8 minutes to roast.

Remove from the oven and allow to rest on the breast side for at least 5 minutes. The breasts are then ready to be carved off to present on the plate.

For the barley

After washing to remove the excess starch, blanch the barley until just cooked and drain before adding to a pan with the chicken stock. Heat, season, then add the butter, chopped truffle and a little lemon juice to taste.

For the sauce

Reduce the Madeira and port to a sryup and pour over the stock along with the thyme and bay leaf, allowing to cook out before passing through a muslin cloth and reducing to a consistency of your liking.

To serve

Place the barley on the plate topped with the quail, then garnish with the beetroots and finish off the dish with a parsley root cream, baby red onions and some of the sauce.

CELERY AND RHUBARB SORBET

SERVES 4

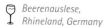 *Beerenauslese,*
Rhineland, Germany

Method

For the sorbet

Place the rhubarb and all the ingredients except the celery juice into a pan and cook them until the rhubarb breaks down, then cool and add the celery juice. Freeze in an ice cream machine.

For the vanilla mousse

Whisk the cream cheese with icing sugar and vanilla, and then heat a little cream to dissolve the gelatin in. Whisk the cream until soft whipped then fold together.

To serve

Garnish with poached rhubarb pieces, cinnamon crisps and fresh strawberries, wild if possible.

At Fraiche we also add candied celery leaves.

Ingredients

Sorbet

300g of rhubarb (peeled and chopped)
30ml liquid glucose
70g caster sugar
25ml Grenadine
150g water
50ml celery juice

Vanilla Mousse

70g cream cheese
20g icing sugar
1g of gelatin
7ml cream
1 vanilla pod (seeded)
1 tsp of vanilla extract

080
FREEMASONS AT WISWELL

8 Vicarage Fold, Wiswell, Clitheroe, Lancashire BB7 9DF

01254 822 218
www.freemasonsatwiswell.com

In just over a year, Freemasons at Wiswell has become one of the shining lights on the Northern culinary stage. Under the creative and accomplished direction of chef-patron Steven Smith, this village country pub, set in the picturesque Ribble Valley countryside, has attracted a loyal regional following as well as growing acclaim within the industry.

Steven's touch in the kitchen is adventurous and assured. His modern interpretations of traditional country dishes feature the finest and freshest ingredients, sourced both locally and from further afield. A seasonal menu is changed regularly to reflect the availability of the very best produce.

Steven said: "We aim to provide a true gastronomic experience but in a relaxed, stylish yet homely pub setting. I am always looking for new flavour combinations, without producing a dish that is too complex. Our staff are friendly and attentive but without being too formal, and as a team we aim to create a memorable dining experience."

With a wine list chosen by experts to match the ever-evolving menu and a recently opened School of Cuisine, Steven and his team aim to build on their early successes, such as the recently awarded Michelin Bib Gourmand, and reach new heights in the coming year.

Steven Smith was recently named Best Newcomer in The Publican awards and Freemasons at Wiswell was ranked in the top 15 gastropubs in the UK

Freemasons Photography by Lottiedesigns.com

TANDOORI ROAST MONKFISH – PIG'S TROTTER NUGGETS AND SCRATCHING, SWEET POTATO, APPLE AND CUMIN

SERVES 4

🍷 *Penny's Viognier 2009, South Africa*

Ingredients

Monkfish

4 monkfish tails
2 tbsp tandoori powder

Potato

2 sweet potatoes

Pig's Trotter

5 pig's trotters
aromats – thyme, garlic, bay leaves,
coriander seed and fennel seed
200g spinach
2 shallots (diced)
1 clove garlic

Cumin Sauce

250g cumin seeds
250ml fish stock
coriander cress
4g lecithin

2 Granny Smith apples

Method

For the monkfish

Trim and clean the monkfish tails and dust them evenly with tandoori powder. Roll into cylinders and poach at 58°C for 20 minutes, then roast until golden.

For the potato

Bake the sweet potatoes in tin foil until soft and caramelised, then scoop the potato flesh out and puree until smooth.

For the pig's trotters

Braise the pig's trotters in water for 4 hours with aromats. When cooked, pick off the meat and dice. Reduce the cooking liqueur by half. Sweat the diced shallots, garlic and cold trotters, then add the reduced cooking liqueur and reduce until sticky. Finish with a chiffonade of raw spinach. Check seasoning. Press into a half terrine mould. When cooked, dice and breadcrumb then deep fry until golden.

For the cumin sauce

Toast cumin seeds to release their flavour naturally and then add the fish stock. Reduce by half, then add milk and bring to boil. Add lecithin and adjust seasoning. Keep warm.

To serve

Serve with sweet potato puree, raw apple and coriander salad.

GOOSNARGH DUCK – POACHED AND ROAST BREAST, LEG MEAT WONTONS, BEETROOT AND ORANGE

SERVES 4

 Jean Grivot Bourgogne
Pinot Noir 2007

Ingredients

Duck

4 white duck breasts

Beetroot

2 x 750ml beetroot juice
750ml apple juice
100ml white wine vinegar
10g agar-agar

Wontons

½ chicken breast
375ml cream
2 duck legs
8 wonton skins

Oranges

4 Seville oranges
Grand Marnier stock syrup

Cabbage

1 Savoy cabbage
cream

Method

For the duck

Trim the ducks and render the skins until golden and crisp, then cool. When cold, vac-pack and poach at 58°C for 45 minutes and recrisp. Rest for 5 minutes.

For the beetroot puree

Reduce with the first 750ml of beetroot juice with the apple juice and 100ml of white wine vinegar, then refresh with the other 750ml serving of beetroot juice. Set with 10g agar-agar.

When cold, puree until smooth.

For the wontons

Blend the chicken breast with the leg and a half pint of cream. Add the confit duck legs and pipe this mixture into the wonton skins. Seal the edges with a little water and deep fry until golden.

For the oranges

Peel and segment the oranges and pour over the Grand Marnier stock syrup.

For the cabbage

Shred fine and braise in cream until soft.

To serve

Slice duck and serve on cabbage and oranges. Top with crispy wontons.

MANGO RAVIOLI, RICE PUDDING AND BLOOD ORANGE SOUP

SERVES 4

🍷 *Tamar Ridge Botrytis Riesling 2008, Tasmania, Australia*

Ingredients

Rice Pudding

215g pudding rice
1.75 litre milk
vanilla pod
sugar to taste
orange zest

Blood Orange Soup

200g blood orange puree
50g stock syrup
zest and juice of 2 blood oranges
1 mango (or enough to line the inside of the mould)

Method

For the rice pudding

Using a knife, remove the vanilla from the pod and place into a pan, then add the milk and pudding rice. Bring to the boil. Once boiled, lower the heat and simmer until the pudding rice is cooked.

Once cooked, add the zest of a blood orange and sugar to taste. Then leave to cool.

For the blood orange soup

Put the syrup, juice and zest of the blood oranges in a blender and blitz. Pass through a sieve and place into a pouring jug to serve.

Line a mould with thinly sliced mango and fill with the rice pudding.

Fold over the thinly sliced mango at the top of the mould to seal then chill in the fridge overnight.

To serve

Carefully remove the mango ravioli from the mould onto a plate.

Serve with segments of fresh blood orange and the blood orange soup.

Finish with fresh coriander.

090
THE INN AT WHITEWELL

Near Clitheroe, Lancashire BB7 3AT

01200 448 222
www.innatwhitewell.com

Based in the beautiful Forest of Bowland, designated an area of Outstanding Natural Beauty, The Inn sits high on the banks of the River Hodder and commands breathtaking views down the valley and sweeping fells to the moors above. The Inn at Whitewell is an increasingly rare thing, a proper rural inn. This listed building dates back to the 1400's is stuffed full of antiques and old sporting art. There are 23 bedrooms, all glamorous, some with gorgeous antique cabinet baths and others with real peat fires.

Whether you come to fish for sea trout or salmon, walk the dogs, read the papers or sample the extensive wine stocked by the in house vintners; wellies, high heels, dogs and children all meld together to create a unique and very relaxing atmosphere. The Inn deservedly has a good reputation and many awards for its food. Head Chef Jamie Cadman, now in his fourteenth year, runs a crew of ten, ably supported by his two Sous Chefs, Gemma and James, producing brilliant local food. His ethos is to use only the best of local ingredients, cooked simply to let the real quality shine through. Seasonal grouse from Lancashire Moor, pheasant and partridge from Dunsop shoot, Bowland beef and Lonk lamb from Burholme Farm are staples on the menu, all easily seen from the Inn's windows.

For a chef to spend over 10 years in the same place is very rare, but for Head Chef Jamie Cadman it can be put down to having a fantastic team behind him, some of which have been with him almost from day one

BRAISED OXTAIL, SHALLOTS IN BEER, POTATO PUREE

SERVES 4

De Colette 'Les Charme de Colette'
Morgon 2009

Method

For the oxtails

Marinade the oxtails with all the other ingredients except the stock for 24 hours, then add the stock and braise at 120°C for 6 hours, or until the meat falls from the bone. Remove the oxtail, pass the liquid and reduce it by ¾, skimming any fat off the top. Carefully remove the meat from the bones, shred it between your fingers and add it to the cooking liquid.

For the shallots

Add all the ingredients to a pan and gently simmer until all the liquid has disappeared.

For the potato puree

Boil the potatoes until tender and then pass through a ricer with the butter. Mix together and check seasoning.

To serve

Split the oxtail between four 7cm pastry cutters. Top with the potato puree and garnish with the shallots.

Ingredients

Oxtail

1 whole oxtail (cut into pieces)
100g smoked streaky bacon
1 tsp marmite
250ml Guinness
2 carrots (chopped)
1 onion (chopped)
2 bay leaves
2 cloves garlic
2 litre chicken stock
1 inch piece horseradish

Shallots

8 small shallots (peeled whole)
50g demerara sugar
250ml hen harrier bitter
1 blade mace

Potato Puree

2 large Maris Piper potatoes
150g butter

RACK OF LONK LAMB, LAMB BREAST, TOMATO AND CUMIN, ANNA POTATOES

SERVES 4

 Coto de Imaz Gran Reserva 1996, Rioja

Ingredients

Lamb

1 x 8 bone rack of lamb (French trimmed)
1 lamb breast (ribs and cartilage removed)
(Ask your butcher to do this)
2 tsp cumin seeds
500g tinned plum tomatoes
½ red chilli
3 cloves garlic

Anna Potatoes

4 large potatoes (peeled and thinly sliced)
150g melted butter
few sprigs of fresh thyme

Method

You will need to start this the day before.

To prepare the lamb

Take the lamb breasts and lay them flat, skin-side down, and sprinkle with 1 tsp cumin seeds and 1 clove of thinly sliced garlic. Season with a little salt and black pepper then roll into a sausage shape and tie it in about four places for it to hold its shape. Place in a casserole dish and add the rest of the garlic, cumin seeds, tomatoes, chilli and enough water to barely cover the lamb. Cook with a lid at 120°C for about 4 hours.

When ready, remove the lamb and allow it to cool slightly, then remove the string and wrap the lamb tightly in clingfilm, forming an even cylinder. Place this in the fridge ready for the next day. Pass the sauce through a sieve and chill.

For the anna potatoes

Layer the potatoes in a cast iron frying pan, brushing the melted butter on each layer and adding the thyme. Then bake at 180°C for 25-35 minutes, just until the edges become crispy. Cut into wedges.

For the lamb

Seal and season the lamb rack and roast for 12-15 minutes at 170°C until pink. Then allow to rest for at least 15 minutes. Slice the lamb breast into twelve 1cm rounds and put under a hot grill until crispy. Remove any fat from the top of the tomato sauce and keep warm.

Carve the lamb rack into 8 cutlets and serve.

To serve

Assemble as in the picture.

VANILLA CUSTARD POTS WITH LEMON SHORTBREAD

SERVES 8

🍷 *Agricola Azienda Inama Vulcaia Apres Vino Dolce 2006 – Veneto, Italy*

Ingredients

Vanilla Custard Pots

2 litres double cream
8 egg yolks
110g caster sugar
2 vanilla pods

Shortbread

300g flour (plain)
200g butter (unsalted)
100g icing sugar
zest 2 lemons

Strawberries

100g strawberries (cut into halves)
2 tsp caster sugar
1 tsp vodka
zest and juice of half an orange
few twists of the black pepper mill

Method

For the vanilla custard pots

Split the vanilla pods and scrape out the seeds, then add them to the yolks and sugar. Put the pods into the cream. Beat the yolks and sugar together until almost white, then gently bring the cream to the boil. Pour this onto the egg yolks and mix well, then put back into the pan and, on a gentle heat, stir with a wooden spoon until it starts to thicken slightly, but do not boil. Pass through a sieve then into your ramekins. Chill for about two hours.

For the shortbread

Cream the sugar and butter together until soft, then add the flour and zest and lightly mix them together. Rest for about 30 minutes then roll it out and cut into fingers or rounds. Bake for about 8 minutes at 180°C or just until they start to colour. When they are cooked, take them out of the oven and dust with caster sugar.

For the strawberries

Mix all the ingredients together and leave at room temperature for 2 hours before serving.

To serve

Serve warm with the custard pots.

LA MOUETTE AT THE ROYAL HILBRE

The Royal Hilbre Boutique Hotel and Spa, 8 Meols Drive, Hoylake, Wirral CH47 4AQ

07581 263 837
www.royalhilbrehotelspa.co.uk

Originally built in 1893 as a grand private Victorian residence, the Royal Hilbre Boutique Hotel and Spa dates back to the mid 1700's. Set in its own grounds, it is just a stone's throw from one of the area's most beautiful beaches at Hilbre Island.

The hotel has been through an extensive refurbishment. Restored to its former glory, it is both opulent and refined. The bedrooms feature hand-carved beds and the bathrooms bear roll-top baths and deluge showers. The hotel also has a six room Spa treatment facility in a dedicated wing of the building, providing the finest spa experiences for its clientele.

The La Mouette Restaurant is run by Marc and Claire Lara. Marc was previously head chef at The London Carriage Works. Claire was MasterChef The Professionals Winner 2010. Before MasterChef, Claire had travelled and worked in both Belgium and France, leaving Liverpool at the tender age of 19 to work in Paris for 5 years. In 2004 she returned home and began to teach cooking at a local college before winning her place as the MasterChef champion. Claire says, 'I learned so much in France about the food and eating and life in general. I am so happy to be opening up a restaurant where I grew up. I've seen fantastic produce everywhere in France and now I see it on the Wirral". The style of food is Modern European, with a seasonal based menu, using only the best locally sourced ingredients.

"There is no secret to our food, just fantastic produce that is simply cooked using plenty of salt and butter!".
If you are seeking a truly indulgent experience, then look no further.

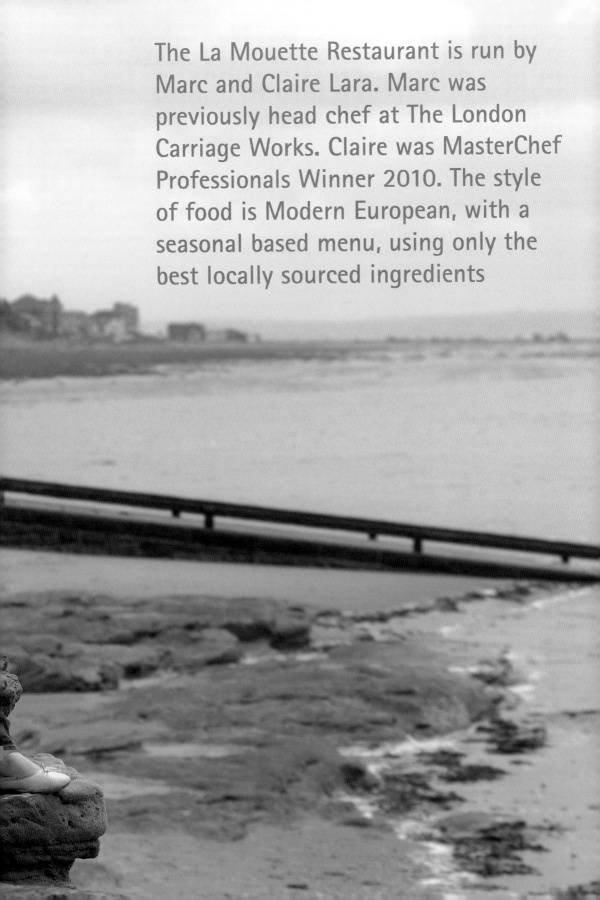

The La Mouette Restaurant is run by Marc and Claire Lara. Marc was previously head chef at The London Carriage Works. Claire was MasterChef Professionals Winner 2010. The style of food is Modern European, with a seasonal based menu, using only the best locally sourced ingredients

SPIDER CRAB SALAD, TOMATO JELLY, CURED CUCUMBER AND AVOCADO MOUSSE

SERVES 6

Macon Charnay 2010 Cuvée a l'Ancienne Burgandy France

Ingredients

Crab and Court Bouillon

2 spider crabs
1 large carrot
4 banana shallots
1 large stick of celery
1 leek
3 star anise
3 bay leaves

Avocado Mousse

4 ripe avocados
400ml double cream
salt and pepper
1 lemon
2 leaves of gelatine

Crab Mix

1 large red pepper
1 large yellow pepper
1/4 bunch of coriander, 1 red chilli
3 tbsp of mayonnaise
salt and pepper, lemon juice

Cured Cucumber and Tomato

1 ripe plum tomato, 1 cucumber
50g of rock salt

Tomato Jelly

6 ripe plum vine tomatoes,
½ cucumber
2 shallots
1 glove of garlic
1 tbsp tomato paste
4 leaves of gelatine (per pint)

Mayonnaise

1 pint of light olive oil
2 egg yolks
1 tsp of mustard
salt and pepper

Method

For the crab

Start by putting all the ingredients into a large pan of boiling water, submerge the crab for 10 to 12 minutes, then remove and cool in ice water. Pick the crab meat from the shells but go through the meat several times to remove any shell. Keep in the fridge.

For the avocado mousse

Cut the avocado in half, remove the stone and scoop the flesh using a spoon. Place the flesh into a pan with all the other ingredients. Boil very quickly and mix with a blender until smooth. Keep in the fridge.

For the cured cucumber

Peel a tomato using a blow torch, remove the centre and cut into neat cubes. Peel and cut the flesh of the cucumber into cubes, the same size as the tomato. Add rock salt and place into a freezer for two hours. Remove and wash them thoroughly under water to remove the salt.

For the tomato jelly

Soak the gelatine in ice cold water. Place all ingredients into a bowl then blend. Pass through muslin and add the gelatine. Add the mix into a tray and refrigerate to set.

For the mayonnaise

Separate the eggs, place yolks into a bowl and spoon in the mustard. Season with salt and slowly whisk in the oil.

To assemble

Blow torch the skin of the peppers until blackened and rub off the skin under a running tap then cut into brunoise (or small dice). Then finely chop the coriander and the red chilli. Add the crab and all the remaining ingredients into a bowl. Bind the mix with the mayonnaise. Adding some salt and pepper to taste.

To serve

Dress all the ingredients onto the plate as in picture.

HERB CRUSTED SPRING LAMB, BRAISED NEW SEASON ONION STUFFED WITH OFFAL, RATATOUILLE AND RED WINE JUS

SERVES 4

Emiliana Réserve Pinot Noir 2009 Chile

Ingredients

Lamb

1 x 1.5kg saddle of lamb on the bone (deboned and trimmed)
250g of broad beans

Lamb Jus

½ bottle of red wine
4 large shallots
2 large carrots
1 stick of celery
1 head of garlic
2 bay leaves, 3 sprigs of thyme,
2 sprigs of rosemary
50g of butter

Stuffed Onions

4 large, new season onions, lamb stock, butter

Stuffing

50g shallots (peeled and finely sliced)
50g lamb kidney
50g lamb's liver
50g of sweetbreads
10g of parsley (finely chopped)

Ratatouille

100g of courgettes
100g of red, yellow and green pepper
100g aubergine
100g red onion
2 cloves of garlic, 1 bay leaf, thyme, rosemary
100g of tomato pulp

Herb Crust

100g fresh breadcrumbs
50g of butter
1 clove of garlic
50g of sage, 100g of parsley, 10g of thyme
100g of chive
100g of parmesan

Method

For the lamb jus

Place all lamb bones and diced lamb trimmings into a heavy roasting tray along with all the peeled and roughly chopped vegetables. Place this in an oven at 190°C until everything on the tray is caramelised. Drain off the fat. Empty the contents of the tray into a stock pot and cover with water. Deglaze the remains in the roasting tray with red wine. Then add to the stock pot with herbs. Boil then simmer for 6 hours, skimming any impurities from the surface. Then discard of bones and vegetables. Pass the stock through a muslin cloth to ensure a perfect shine and season.

For the stuffed onions

Remove the outer skin and place into a heavy bottomed saucepan and cover with lamb stock and butter. Cover and braise in a moderate oven until tender. Once the large, new season onions are out of the oven, allow them to cool.

For the stuffing

Fry the shallots in rapeseed oil until tender. Add a splash of balsamic vinegar then season and allow to cool. Next, remove the sinew from kidneys, liver and sweetbreads. Roll the offal mix in seasoned flour and fry quickly in a very hot pan. Place on absorbent paper then finely chop it. Add parsley and some reduced sauce with balsamic onions. Now you can stuff the onions. Slice the top off and fill them, firstly with the balsamic onions and followed by the sticky offal. Put the top back on and dress.

For the ratatouille

Dice the vegetables and fry off in oil and butter. Add tomato pulp, simmer gently and season.

For the herb crust

Place all the ingredients into a food processor. When the mixture is smooth, place between two sheets of silicone paper. Flatten with a rolling pin and then allow it to set hard in the fridge. Cut it to size when it is set.

For the lamb

Remove the lamb from the fridge and season on both sides. Heat up a pan and seal the lamb on both sides until coloured. Next, place the lamb in an oven at 180°C for 8 to 10 minutes then remove and top with a square of the herb crust. Warm up your ratatouille and reheat your onion in the oven. Then place your lamb back into the oven for a further 4 minutes. Reheat your sauce and bring everything together at the same time.

To serve

Dress the plate accordingly and assemble as in picture.

STRAWBERRY DELICE WITH DACQUOISE BISCUIT, STRAWBERRY JELLY AND MOUSSE, WHITE CHOCOLATE AND JUNIPER ICE CREAM

SERVES 4

 Tabali Late Harvest Muscat 2009 Chile

Ingredients

Dacquoise Biscuit

80g ground almonds
2 x 50g caster sugar
15g plain flour
3 medium egg whites

Strawberry Jelly

500g strawberries
80g of caster sugar
½ lemon
5 to 6 leaves of gelatine

Strawberry Mousse

500g strawberries
200ml of double cream

White Chocolate

200g of white chocolate

Juniper Ice Cream

250ml of whole milk
250ml double cream
3 egg yolks
70g caster sugar
15g juniper berries

Garnish

100g large strawberries

Method

For the biscuits

Mix the ground almond with 50g of the caster sugar and flour. Beat the egg whites with the remaining 50g of caster sugar until it stiffens. Combine the two mixtures and spread onto silicone paper. Bake for 15 minutes at 180°C. Leave it to cool and then cut into required shapes.

For the jelly

Add the strawberries, sugar and the juice of ½ a lemon into a bowl. Place on top of a pan with water and infuse the strawberries for one hour. Pass the mix through muslin and add some gelatine to the liqueur (keep 20ml of liqueur for the sauce). Set on a tray in your fridge.

For the mousse

Mix the strawberries in a blender and pass through a fine chinois. Add whipped double cream and add the strawberry puree to it. Place in the fridge to chill.

For the white chocolate

Temper the white chocolate and spray onto silicone paper. Once the white chocolate is tempered, leave in a cool place rather than in the fridge and cut to size when cold.

For the ice cream

Place cream and milk into a saucepan along with the juniper berries. Boil at this stage and remove the pan from the heat. Cover the pan with clingfilm (this will help the juniper infuse into the cream and milk). After a few minutes remove the clingfilm and sieve out the juniper. Warm the cream and milk mixture.

Next, mix the yolks and sugar and pour them over the cream and milk mixture. Return to the pan and cook until it reaches 85°C. Then pass one last time through a sieve and into a paco jet container.

Freeze and churn just before serving.

To serve

Slice the strawberries for decoration. Build the cake into different layers. Once you have built the layers ball the ice cream and enjoy.

110
THE LAWNS RESTAURANT

Thornton Hall, Neston Road, Thornton Hough, Wirral CH63 1JF

0151 336 3938
www.lawnsrestaurant.co.uk

Thornton Hall is the finest hotel in the Wirral and one of Merseyside's premier venues. Based in the beautiful village of Thornton Hough, close to the Cheshire border, it offers the highest quality of accommodation and facilities with customer service to match.

The four star, family owned Thornton Hall Hotel & Spa has built up a fine reputation for service and hospitality, providing excellent food and drinks in the award-winning Lawns Restaurant and luxurious accommodation in 63 bedrooms and suites.

The Lawns is a multiple AA Rosette winning restaurant and the highest scoring restaurant in The Mersey Partnership's Taste Liverpool scheme – scoring a record 91 per cent.

Executive Chef David Gillmore has launched a private dining experience in the stunning Oak Room with an exclusive menu, as well as a special seven course 'Tasting Menu' with dishes such as Hand Dived Scallops and Cheshire Provencal Lamb.

The Lawns prides itself on sourcing the best local produce and ingredients and has spent £160,000 on refurbishments to create a premiere fine dining experience.

Chef David, who has previously worked at the Michelin starred restaurants The Grosvenor Hotel in Chester and The Vineyard in Berkshire, can also create bespoke menus for all private dining needs.

Executive Chef David Gillmore has launched a private dining experience in the stunning Oak Room with an exclusive menu, as well as a special seven course 'Tasting Menu' with dishes such as Hand Dived Scallops and Cheshire Provencal Lamb

CURED SALMON, JERSEY ROYAL POTATOES & 55 MINUTE EGG YOLK

SERVES 4

🍷 *Maison Champy, Chablis 1er cru Burgundy, France 2008*

Ingredients

Salmon
4 x 80g salmon filets (skinless)
100g cooking salt
1 litre cold water

55 Minute Egg Yolks
4 eggs

Potato Crisps
1 Maris Piper potato

Potato Salad
300g Jersey Royal potatoes
mayonnaise
2 tsp chives (chopped)

Asparagus and Puree
8 pieces asparagus
4 pieces white asparagus

Garnish
4 Nasturtium flowers
rock salt

Method

For the salmon

Dissolve the salt in the water and place the salmon pieces in this solution for 3 hours. Remove the salmon from the solution and rinse it under cold, running tap water for 5 minutes. Set an electronic steamer to 45°C and cook the salmon for 20 minutes. Chill and keep refrigerated until ready to serve.

For the potato salad

Wash the potatoes and then boil them in salted water until tender. When they are cooked, drain and leave to cool. When cold, crush the potatoes and mix them with mayonnaise and chives. Taste for seasoning and adjust accordingly.

For the asparagus and puree

Trim the ends of the asparagus and reserve them. Cut the asparagus to 2 inches in length. Peel the white asparagus, but only peel the green asparagus if it is thick in diameter. Cook in boiling, salted water and refresh in ice water.

Chop the trimmings from the green asparagus and cook in boiling, salted water until soft. Place in a blender and blend to a smooth puree.

For the 55 minute egg yolks

Place the whole eggs into a water bath at 65°C and cook for 55 minutes. Remove and keep in a warm place once cooked.

For the potato crisps

Peel and thinly slice a potato, then coat it in clarified butter and place on greaseproof paper. Cook it between two heavy baking trays at 150°C until golden brown.

To serve

Put some potato salad into a ring and place the salmon on top. Drag lines of asparagus puree across a plate and arrange the white and green asparagus on top. Peel an egg and remove all the white, then season the yolk with rock salt and place into centre of the asparagus tips. Garnish with potato crisps and nasturtium flowers.

FILLET OF BRILL, WILD MUSHROOMS, WIRRAL OXTAIL & PARSLEY PEARLS

SERVES 4

🍷 *Gevrey Chambertin "Vieilles Vignes"*
France 2007

Ingredients

4 x 150g brill fillet (skinless)

Oxtail

1kg oxtail
1 litre veal stock

Onions

12 baby onions
400ml duck fat

Mushroom Puree

500g button mushroom
300ml whipping cream

Parsley Pearls

300g curly parsley
8g calcium lactate
1.5g xanthum gum
500ml water
4g sodium alginate

Wild Mushrooms

200g mixed wild mushrooms (girolles, morels, St.Georges)

Method

For the oxtail

Fry the oxtail pieces in hot oil and place in the veal stock. Cover the container in tin foil and cook in the oven at 120°C until the meat falls away from the bone. Allow about 3 hours for this to happen. Remove the oxtail from the liquid then reduce the stock to create the sauce. Remove meat from bone, trying to keep it in large pieces.

For the onions

Peel the baby onions and place them into a saucepan, then cover with duck fat and cook over a low heat until soft.

For the mushrooms puree

Clean and slice the button mushrooms, then sweat them off until all liquid has been evaporated from them. Add the cream, bring to the boil and then puree in a blender until smooth. Check seasoning and adjust accordingly.

For the parsley pearls

Plunge the curly parsley into boiling water and cook until soft. Refresh in iced water then squeeze out any excess water and puree in a blender until smooth. Add calcium lactate and xanthum gum to puree and bring to the boil.

Mix water and sodium alginate, over a medium heat, but do not boil.

Dip a half teaspoon measuring spoon into the alginate bath, then scoop a measurement of parsley puree and drop into the bath. Leave for 3 minutes until a coating has formed. Remove from the bath and rinse in a bowl of warm water to remove any excess alginate mixture. Stir in some thin parsley puree.

For the wild mushrooms

Trim and wash all of the mushrooms and sauté them in some butter until soft.

To serve

When just about to serve, poach the brill fillet until opaque, re-heat the mushroom puree and sauté off the wild mushrooms along with the drained onions. Reheat the oxtail meat in the reduced sauce and add chopped parsley. Reheat the parsley pearls in some of the thin puree and plate as in the picture.

MILK CHOCOLATE MOUSSE, PASSION FRUIT AND YOGHURT SORBET

SERVES 4

 Laurent Perrier
Demi Sec

Ingredients

Mousse

90ml water
95g sugar
4 egg yolks
200g milk chocolate
400ml whipping cream (whipped to soft peaks)

Chocolate Collar

200g dark chocolate

Passion Fruit Sauce

200ml passion fruit puree
60g caster sugar
1 tsp cornflour
1 tsp water
1 passion fruit

Frozen Chocolate Powder

50g dark chocolate
30g cocoa
30g caster sugar
100ml whipping cream
150ml water

Yoghurt Sorbet

250ml milk
250ml natural yoghurt
165g caster sugar

Method

For the mousse

Whisk egg yolks until pale and increased in volume (preferably on an electric machine), then boil sugar and water to 118°C (known as soft ball). Once this temperature is reached, pour sugar mix onto the yolks gradually and continue whisking. Add the melted chocolate to the egg mix and beat in until all the chocolate is incorporated into the mix. Then fold in the softly whipped cream. Pour into rings and place in the freezer until frozen.

For the chocolate collar

Melt the chocolate at 45°C, leave to cool to 27°C and then warm back up to 30°C (this is to temper the chocolate to produce a crisp collar around the mousse). Spread the tempered chocolate onto acetate strips so that it is about 3mm thick, and then wrap the acetate around the mousse to form a collar. Place mousses into fridge until set and ready to serve.

For the passion fruit sauce

Boil the puree and sugar. Separately, mix the cornflour and water, then add this to the puree mixture and return to the boil. Remove from heat, add passion fruit seeds and refrigerate until needed.

For the frozen chocolate powder

Heat all ingredients until the dry goods have dissolved and the chocolate has melted. Then pour into a container and freeze until solid.

For the yoghurt sorbet

Mix ingredients together and churn in an ice cream machine until frozen. Place into a container and place in freezer until needed.

To serve

Assemble as in the picture.

120
THE LONDON CARRIAGE WORKS

Hope Street, Liverpool L1 9DA

0151 705 2222
www.thelondoncarriageworks.co.uk

Convivial is one of Paul Askew's favourite words and The London Carriage Works is run on the maxim to create and enjoy a roomful of conviviality; the design, the staff and service, the aspect, our neighbours and not least the delicious food and memorable wines all working together.

Two walls of windows look out onto one of the most culturally and architecturally exciting streets in Britain. The restaurant has some pretty inspiring neighbours, all within a five minute walk; the Victoria Gallery & Museum (University's eclectic collection), Liverpool Metropolitan Cathedral (the Catholics), Everyman Theatre (National treasure), Philharmonic Hall (home to the Royal Liverpool Philharmonic Orchestra), Unity theatre (New writers), Hardman House (National Trust goody), Liverpool Cathedral (the Anglicans)... exhausted? Well, throw in a fantastic selection of restaurants and three serious ale houses and we're almost there!

Named after the original 1864 company (it did what it said on the can), The London Carriage Works opened in 2004 as a restaurant to the boutique hope street hotel, both brands immediately becoming a winning partnership for weddings, events and celebrations. Locally the restaurant is a destination in its own right, a fantastic symbol of Liverpool's renaissance not only as a place to visit but to eat!

The London Carriage Works is a room of elegance and style, a fitting counter point to Paul Askew and his team's ethos to be unpretentious and honest about their dishes, wanting to deliver the very best flavours and textures that come from the season, the farms, the coastlines and seas.

There is the most geeky excitement when the 'firsts' of a season arrive, the buzz is palatable around the building! Wirral watercress, Bowland beef, Liverpool Bay sea bass, Southport samphire, Claremont farm asparagus and Callum Edge's lamb, all ingredients for a wonderful night out watching the wonderful world go by.

The flavours you encounter through life trigger strong memories and feelings, this is what our chefs and waiters are keen to deliver; those flavour memories that will stay with you and bring you back to us time and time again

KING SCALLOP WITH BRAISED PORK CHEEK AND MORCILLA, SERVED WITH CAULIFLOWER PUREE, GOLDEN RAISIN DRESSING AND JUS

SERVES 4

🍷 *Finca de Arantei, Albarino*
The best of British meets Spain

Ingredients

4 large king scallops in shells (cleaned)
4 slices of "morcilla" Spanish black pudding
A little butter

Pork Cheeks

4 pork cheeks
1 carrot (washed, peeled and diced)
1 stick of celery (washed, peeled and diced)
1 medium onion (peeled and diced)
50ml cider (Organic Westerns)
5 sprigs of thyme
150ml brown stock
50ml chardonnay vinegar
50ml fino sherry

Puree

1 sputna potato (peeled and washed)
1 small cauliflower - trimmed and washed
100g butter
6 garlic cloves (peeled)
50ml double cream
salt and pepper

Dressing

50ml vegetable oil
50g golden raisins
1 large shallot – peeled and diced
salad
frisee lettuce
Sorrel
1 Granny Smith apple

TLCW jus

(you'll have to come to The London Carriage Works for that!) - commercial tetra packs of jus are available from supermarkets

Method

This is a beautiful, complex dish and one of my favourites with six main elements and a little salad to garnish.

For the pork cheek

Trim all the outside sinew off the pork cheek leaving a clean piece of meat.

In a hot pan, season and seal the meat until golden brown all over.

Then put the root vegetables, cider, stock and herbs into ovenproof earthenware and cook for 4 hours on gas mark three until tender (Long and slow!).

Strain the cooking liquor and reduce until jus consistency. Vac-pack the cheeks, individually with a little sauce, in each. Reheat in a water bath to serve.

For the puree

Cook the potato, cauliflower and three cloves of garlic in salted water with 100g butter until soft (about 20 minutes). Liquidise whilst hot (be careful!) and spoon the mixture into the jug of the blender with a little liquor and a splash of cream. Season and then blend until smooth.

For the dressing

Warm the golden raisins and diced shallots in a pan with a splash of oil and seasoning. Add some of the 50ml of chardonnay vinegar and some of the 50ml of dry sherry (to taste) and reduce by half. Leave to cool but serve a little warm.

For the salad

Julienne (thin matchsticks shape) the Granny Smith apple and add some Frisee and sorrel. At the last minute, dress with olive oil and vinegar.

To assemble the dish

Warm the puree and pork cheeks.

Have a hot, oiled, thick-bottomed sauté pan ready for the scallop. Place the scallop presentation-side down in the hot oiled pan along with a sprinkling of sea salt. Allow to caramelise until golden brown before turning. Then add the morcilla and a knob of butter before finishing. (Cooking the scallop and morcilla should be no longer than 2-3 minutes).

To serve

Put a spoonful or two of puree on each plate as per the photograph. Then place the scallop, morcilla and cheek on the puree in a line for neatness of presentation. Add the salad and a tablespoon of dressing, followed by a little jus to finish. Enjoy!

JOHN DORY WITH SOUTHPORT SAMPHIRE, CLAREMONT FARM ASPARAGUS, POMMES VIOLETTE, CARROT PUREE AND CRAB BISQUE

SERVES 4

 Sancerre, Domaine Michel Girard

Ingredients

1 x 2kg large John Dory fish (filleted and portioned by your fishmonger - retain the bones for stock)

8 purple potatoes, pommes violette (washed and parboiled)

200g samphire (picked and washed)

8 green and 8 white Claremont Farm asparagus spears (peeled and washed)

4 carrots (washed peeled and roughly cut)

1 large spunta or paris piper potato (washed and peeled)

4 cloves garlic

100g unsalted butter

50ml double cream

pinch of Maldon sea salt, white pepper, caster sugar

pure vegetable oil for sauté

Bisque

(makes enough for this dish and a bit more to drink like elixir)

Dory bones

3kg Fresh Filey crab shells (from the fishmonger, roasted for 10 minutes in a hot oven 180°C)

4 or 5 ripe vine tomatoes cut in half

1 bulb of garlic split in half

4 sticks celery, 2 carrots, 1 onion (all roughly chopped)

100g parsley stalks

½ lemon

4 bay leaves

100g thyme

50ml cognac

10g butter

1 pint cream

6 peppercorns

seasoning to taste

Method

Like all good restaurant dishes this is all about the quality of the ingredients and the advance preparation, so this method starts with the items that can be done the day before or morning of the dinner party.

For the bisque

First make a stock using the Dory bones and roasted crab bones, garlic, herbs, vegetables and lemon. Cover the ingredients with cold water, bring to the boil and simmer for 4 hours. Skim off any impurities with a ladle along the way. Strain the liquid by passing it through a muslin cloth, then reduce it through boiling by half. Then add the cognac, cream and butter, bringing it back to the boil and whisk as we go until thickened and of pouring consistency. Whisk in a little more butter at the end if necessary. Adjust the seasoning to taste, including a pinch of sugar if balance is required. This can be chilled and reheated as required or kept warm for service.

For the puree

Put the carrots, potato and garlic into a pan with salted cold water and 50g butter. Simmer until the vegetables are cooked soft. When still hot, spoon the vegetables and a little of the liquid into a liquidiser. Seasoning and adding a little butter and cream along the way.

For the dish itself

Parboil the potatoes and cut in half ready to sauté. Prepare the asparagus and samphire. Use a hot thick bottomed sauté pan for the fish and potatoes. Get three pans on the heat. One for the Dory, one for the potatoes and a saucepan with seasoned water and butter (bring to the boil). Place potatoes face down in a hot pan with a little oil and sea salt.

For the john dory

Add the Dory skin-side down in the oiled pan with a little sea salt. Allow these to begin to brown. The skin of the fish should be golden brown like autumn leaves. Turn, add butter and leave off the heat to finish cooking. This takes 3 to 4 minutes in total. Use the same technique for the purple potatoes.

While these items are finishing drop the asparagus and samphire into the water for 1 minute.

Take all the items and drain onto kitchen paper before plating.

To serve

Dress as in picture and finish with watercress or pea shoots.

Enjoy!

CHOCOLATE MARQUISE WITH PLUM SORBET AND CHOCOLATE TUILE

SERVES 4

 Antique Pedro Ximenez (deliciously sweet sherry)

Ingredients

Genoise

25g cocoa
4 eggs
125g caster sugar
100g flour

Chocolate Mousse

4 egg whites
140g caster sugar
150ml water
400g of 53% chocolate
120ml milk
120ml cream
400ml cream whipped to ribbon consistency

Brandy Syrup

25ml brandy
150g caster sugar
75ml water

Sorbet

250ml water
175ml cranberry juice
80g caster sugar
2 tbsp of glucose syrup
500g Santa Rosa plums (de-stones and de-skinned)
squeeze of lemon
crushed pistachios (to sit the sorbet on and to garnish)

Tuile

75ml orange juice
150g caster sugar
75g unsalted butter
55g sifted plain flour
20g cocoa powder

Method

For the genoise

Whisk the eggs and sugar until tripled in volume.

Sieve the flour and cocoa and fold in gently with the eggs and sugar.

Bake for around 20 minutes at 180°C (gas mark 4) or until firm and a wooden skewer comes out clean.

(My mum used to use a knitting needle!)

For the chocolate mousse

Boil caster sugar and water until it reaches 120°C.

Start to whisk the egg whites with an electric whisk and slowly add the sugar syrup. Continue whisking until whites form a stiff peak and leave to one side.

In another bowl, whisk 400ml cream until it resembles a ribbon consistency and leave to one side.

Melt chocolate in a bain-marie, then boil 120ml milk and 120ml cream and add the melted chocolate and stir gently. Then very gently fold in the meringue and the whipped cream.

For the brandy syrup

Put all into a pan and boil for one minute.

To assemble the marquise

Put the genoise into a gastronom tray lined with silicone paper. Spoon over the brandy syrup followed by a layer one to two inch deep layer of mousse. Leave in the freezer for at least two hours (to maintain shape) before portioning.

For the sorbet

Boil all the ingredients together, then blend, then pass through a sieve and churn until frozen. Put in a deep freeze until ready to use.

For the tuile

Put the orange juice, sugar and butter in a pan and bring to the boil. Add the flour and cocoa and mix thoroughly, chill, then spread onto greaseproof paper and bake at 180°C (gas mark 4) for 5 – 10 minutes or until it starts to bubble on top, take out of the oven. After 30 seconds check if it remains crispy, if not, return to the oven for a further 2 minutes. Once crispy leave to cool then snap into shards for garnish.

To serve

Assemble as in the picture with some seasonal berries.

130
LUNYA

18-20 College Lane, Liverpool One, Liverpool L1 3DS

0151 706 9770
www.lunya.co.uk

Set in the heart of Liverpool in a beautifully converted 18th century warehouse is the unique Catalonian restaurant and deli, Lunya. Wirral based business man Peter Kinsella opened the doors to Lunya in 2010 after a business trip to Barcelona in 1999 saw him fall in love with the city and its food and atmosphere. After many more visits, Peter finally realised his ambition of opening a Catalan deli and restaurant.

As the UK's first Catalonian fusion deli and restaurant, Peter prides himself on sourcing the finest artisan Catalan and Spanish ingredients, as well as the freshest and highest quality local ingredients, to produce the most authentic deli around.

The menu provides a wide range of tapas, paella and wood-oven roasted suckling pig; many based on the concept of fusion - blending recipes, ideas and ingredients from Spain and the UK together. The award-winning chefs believe in making absolutely everything themselves from superb quality ingredients. Quite simply, the dishes are 'passion on a plate'.

The restaurant has a relaxed and atmospheric ambience that easily transcends from the busy breakfast period through to the evening and, fortunately, it is not just Liverpool that benefits, as the in-house deli now delivers its Spanish food nationwide.

Lunya gained critical acclaim within the first year of opening by winning Best Restaurant from Lancashire Life, Cheshire Life and the Liverpool Food Festival, whilst Head Chef Eirian Lunt was named Chef of the Year at the Liverpool Ambassador Awards.

The restaurant has a relaxed and atmospheric ambience that easily transcends from the busy breakfast period through to the evening and, fortunately, it is not just Liverpool that benefits as the in-house deli now delivers its Spanish food nationwide

ENSALADA MARISCO

SERVES 4

🍷 *Cora Loxarel (Chardonnay/Muscat),*
D.O. Penedès

Ingredients

200g crab sticks
100g small prawns (chopped)
4 spring onions (finely chopped)
4 large sprigs parsley (finely chopped)
5 heaped tbsp mayonnaise
juice of half a lemon
salt and pepper
4 tail-on king prawns (optional)
4 spanish breadsticks (optional)

Method

Cut the crab sticks in half and then slice finely length ways.

Add the prawns, spring onion, parsley and lemon juice and mix them gently together.

Add the mayonnaise and mix until everything is evenly covered.

Season to taste.

To serve

Assemble as in the picture. We serve this dish with a tail-on king prawn and picos de pan (small Spanish bread-sticks).

IBÉRICO TENDER LOIN WITH BUBBLE & SQUEAK

SERVES 4

Fuenteseca Bobal Cabernet Sauvignon,
D.O. Utiel-Requena

Ingredients

Pork

1kg Ibérico tenderloin (or regular tender loin if
not available)
100ml Pedro Ximénez sherry
1 litre orange juice
1 tsp of fresh thyme
salt, pepper and sugar to taste
1 tsp of arrowroot

Bubble and Squeak

3 large potatoes
1 large carrot (finely chopped)
100g of shredded spring cabbage
extra virgin olive oil
salt and pepper

Method

For the pork

Marinade the pork in the orange juice, PX sherry and thyme for
24 hours.

Take out the marinade and sear in a pan over a high heat until
just cooked (medium rare if Ibérico tender loin).

Leave to rest, then add the marinade and reduce over a high
heat. Add a little sugar to sweeten the sauce and a little
arrowroot to thicken.

For the bubble and squeak

Boil the peeled and chopped potatoes until just soft, then mash
with the olive oil and salt and pepper until nicely smooth. Add
the cooked chopped carrots and shredded cabbage, mix well and
shape into patties and fry on each side until browned.

To serve

Slice the tender loin into 2cm pieces, arrange over the patty of
bubble and squeak and drizzle the sauce over.

RHUBARB AND MEMBRILLO CRUMBLE

SERVES 4

 *Goya Moscatel Classico*

Ingredients

Rhubarb

200g of rhubarb (about 10 sticks)
60ml of water
150g caster sugar
100g membrillo (quince jelly – chopped into
1cm pieces)

Crumble

110g butter (softened)
110g demerara sugar
180g plain flour
30g almonds (chopped)

Method

For the rhubarb

Preheat the oven to 180°C/350F/Gas 4.

Cut the rhubarb into 5cm long pieces, and place in an oven proof dish.

Add the membrillo and sugar. Mix well and sprinkle with water.

For the crumble

With your hands, rub the butter into the flour and sugar to make the topping, then add the chopped almonds and ensure they are distributed evenly in the mixture.

Sprinkle evenly over the rhubarb mixture and bake for approximately 40 minutes.

To serve

Assemble as in the picture.

Chefs tip

The topping should be crisp and golden.

140 MARITIME DINING ROOMS

Merseyside Maritime Museum, Albert Dock, Liverpool L3 4AQ

0151 478 4499
www.liverpoolmuseums.org.uk

The Maritime Dining Rooms are located on the fourth floor of the grade 1 listed Merseyside Maritime Museum, whose collections reflect the vitality and importance of the Port of Liverpool and its role in world history. The restaurant's dual aspect views are breathtaking, capturing the city's history, renaissance and regeneration. On the south side, diners look out over the busy Albert Dock with its grade 1 listed buildings, ships and boats, whilst the north side of the restaurant overlooks the famous World Heritage site and the new Museum of Liverpool. The contemporary and stylish interior reflects the Art Deco design of the many great luxury liners that have passed through Liverpool.

The restaurant's team are passionate about providing excellent service to diners and delivering great tasting food with skill and flair.

The menu, created by Head Chef Ben Sheeran, celebrates both British and local produce, combining classic flavours with a modern twist. Dishes change regularly to reflect the best seasonal flavours. There are vegetarian and vegan options, a children's menu, an excellent value family meal deal, a comprehensive wine list and a tempting afternoon tea menu.

The Maritime Dining Rooms are one of only ten Liverpool restaurants recommended in the Michelin Guide to Great Britain and Ireland 2010 and 2011.

The menu, created by Head Chef Ben Sheeran, celebrates both British and local produce, combining classic flavours with a modern twist. Dishes change regularly to reflect the best seasonal flavours

BLACK PUDDING, FREE RANGE EGG AND DROP BOTTOM MUFFIN WITH SHEERAN BROWN SAUCE

SERVES 6

 Cains Raisin Beer

Ingredients

Black Pudding

(12 portions)
700g pork belly (diced)
1 litre chicken/pork stock
500g blood (dried)
115g oats
100g pearl barley
2½ green apples (diced leaving skin on)
375g onion (finely diced)
10g mint
12.5g parsley
15g spice mix (equal amounts ground pepper,
ground coriander and clove)

Brown Sauce

450g green apple (quartered leaving skin on)
110g stoned prunes
120g onion (diced)
450ml malt vinegar
225g brown sugar
3g ground ginger
2g ground nutmeg
2g Cayenne pepper

English Muffin

450g strong plain flour
5g salt
225ml milk
5g caster sugar
10g dried yeast
50g butter
55ml water

6 medium sized eggs (boiled)

Method

For the black pudding

Cook the pork belly in a pressure cooker if you have one. If not, just place it in a pan with onions and carrots and boil for around 1hr 30 minutes. Remove the belly pork and retain 1litre of the stock (top up with chicken stock to make 1 litre if required). Leave to cool, then dice into ½ cm cubes. While this is cooking, cover the pearl barley with water and cook until tender. This will take around 20 minutes. While the stock, pork and barley are cooling combine the remaining ingredients in one bowl ready to mix all the elements together. Place in a heat-proof mould or wrap in clingfilm to form a sausage shape and boil it for 25 minutes. The black pudding should reach a temperature of over 80°C when probed to ensure it is cooked through. Once cooked it can be stored in the fridge for 5 days and pan-fried to re-heat.

For the brown sauce

Quarter the apples, dice the onion and add them all to a large pan along with the prunes. Cover with water and cook until tender, then puree. In another pan, add the spices, vinegar and sugar and boil to reduce by a third. Add the apple and prune mix and cook out until it thickens.

For the english muffin

Add the milk and water to a small saucepan and heat until hot. Pour into a jug, then add the sugar and dried yeast mix with a fork and leave for about 10 minutes to get a really frothy head. Sift the flour and salt into a large mixing bowl and make a well in the centre, pour in the yeast mixture and mix to a soft dough – it should leave the bowl cleanly but if it seems a bit sticky add more flour. Knead the dough for about 10 minutes, by which time it should be smooth and elastic. Place the dough back into the bowl, cover it with clingfilm and leave in a warm place until it has doubled in size. This will take about 30 minutes or longer depending on the temperature. When the dough has risen, lightly flour the work surface then roll the dough out to about 1 cm thick. Then, using a 7.5 cm plain cutter, cut out 12 rounds. Place the muffins on a lightly floured baking sheet, sprinkle them with a little more flour and leave them to puff up again for about 25 minutes in a warm place or in an oven on a low heat.

To cook, grease a thick-based frying pan with a trace of oil. Heat the pan and cook them for about 7 minutes. You'll need to do these in 3 or 4 batches but they can be made well in advance. If you want to serve them in the traditional way break them just a little around their waists without opening them then toast lightly on both sides.

To serve

Boil the eggs and remove the shells. Assemble as in picture.

BALLOTINE OF RABBIT WITH RABBIT BON BONS, PUY LENTILS AND PICKLED GIROLLES

SERVES 6

 5th generation unoaked Chardonnay
Australia

Ingredients

3 large rabbits

Ballotine of Rabbit

1 egg white
100ml double cream

Rabbit Bon Bons

salt and pepper
handful of parsley (chopped)
60g butter
fine breadcrumbs
100ml milk
50g flour

Puy Lentils

220g puy lentils
2 cloves garlic
1 onion (finely diced)
3g rosemary
3 sage leaves
350ml red wine
350ml water
handful parsley (chopped)
50ml olive oil

Pickled Girolles

200g Girolle mushrooms
50ml olive oil
1 clove garlic (sliced)
60ml white wine vinegar
30g caster sugar
100g parsley (chopped)
salt and pepper

Carrot Puree

5 carrots (peeled and sliced)
small handful of onion (diced)
500ml double cream
60g butter

Method

For the puy lentils

Heat 50ml of olive oil in a saucepan with 2 cloves of garlic and the onion, sage and rosemary. Add the lentils and cook for 2 minutes so they are coated in oil. Pour in the red wine and reduce the liquid to half. Add water and cook the lentils with a lid on for 20 minutes or until softened. Season with salt and pepper and add a handful of chopped parsley.

For the girolles

Sauté the Girolles in the olive oil with the garlic until brown. Add the sugar, vinegar, chopped parsley and season with salt and pepper.

For the ballotine of rabbit

Take each rabbit and remove the top half by cutting just above the rib cage and just above the back legs so that you are left with the loin and the rib cage. Remove three of the legs and take off the meat, placing it in a food processor with the egg white, then remove as much meat from the top carcass as you can and add it to these. Blend the meat until smooth and just before you turn the processor off add 100ml cream. Then season.

Take a sharp knife, turn the loin on its front and run the tip of the knife down the spine of the rabbit to score the flesh. Turn it back around and place the knife against the spine on the inside, slicing down and putting pressure on the knife on the bone side.

Now remove the loin, keeping the flap of meat that covers the rib cage (you can use this to hold the mousse in). If you were lucky enough to have been given the liver with your rabbit season and lay the liver next to the loin and spread the mousse over the top protecting it from any harsh heat. Roll the rabbit into a sausage shape with clingfilm and poach for 15 minutes in a pan of simmering water. Remove the clingfilm then pan-fry to reheat caramelising the outside.

For the rabbit bon bons

With the other legs and carcasses place them into a pan and cover with water. Cook until the meat is tender enough to be removed. Mix the meat (reserving the stock) with salt, pepper and parsley and make into 6 round balls, then roll in fine breadcrumbs. Shallow fry until golden and crispy.

Reduce the stock by half and monté with butter to finish the dish.

For the carrot puree

Fry the carrots and onion. Add cream and heat until soft. Blend with the 60g of butter.

To serve

Assemble as in the picture.

TONKER BEAN CHEESE CAKE WITH SALT CARAMEL AND POACHED PEACH

SERVES 6

🍷 *Wernddu Farm Welsh Perry*
Medium/Dry

Ingredients

Filling
300g Philadelphia cheese
150g caster sugar
2 tonker beans (grated)
11g gelatine leaves
2tbsp stock syrup (from the poached peach)
200ml whipping cream

Base
150g digestive biscuits (crushed)
50g unsalted butter (melted)

Salt Caramel
10g salt flakes
140g sugar

Poached Peach
3 peaches
1 pint stock syrup

Method

For the poached peach
Make about 1 pint of stock syrup (water and sugar) and poach your peaches in it for 3 minutes, then remove and chill, keeping the stock syrup for the gelatine later.

For the salt caramel
Put the sugar in a pan and heat slowly until it starts to brown, then stir it, take it off the heat and cool on a non-stick tray. When this is cold you can blend it to a powder and keep in the freezer. When you want to use it, take it out of the freezer, mix with the salt and sprinkle evenly on a silicon mat. Bake at 190°C until it melts together and has the required colour (this will take around 4 minutes but don't forget it will be very hot and will keep on cooking when it comes out of the oven).

For the base
Mix the crushed biscuits with the melted butter and press into the base of a lightly greased, 20cm, loose-based cake tin. Leave this to chill in the fridge.

For the filling
Beat together the Philly cheese, sugar and grated tonker beans. Bloom the gelatine in cold water until soft, then squeeze out the water and mix in with the 2tbsp of hot stock syrup. Add this to the cheese mix.

Whip the cream until it is just holding its shape and fold into the Philly mixture. Spoon over the base and level the top. Chill for 2-3 hours or overnight.

To serve
Before serving decorate with broken shards of caramel and half a poached peach.

150
THE MONRO

92 Duke Street, Liverpool L1 5AG

0151 707 9933
www.themonro.com

The focus at The Monro has always been on excellent food. This popular Gastropub was the first in Liverpool and remains the first choice for discerning customers that love the taste of great food. With all the dishes created from scratch, savvy customers know that they'll be able to taste the freshness in the first bite and all this is at surprising wallet friendly prices.

Situated in a delightful converted Grade II listed, former merchant's home, The Monro has been featured on television and is a favourite of the Sunday press being widely featured in The Sunday Times, The Observer and The Independent. The owner William Lyons said, "To maintain its position as number one, the focus has always got to be on the quality, from the quality of ingredients, the service and the surroundings. From all this the whole customer experience will follow".

Judging by the constantly bustling atmosphere, The Monro welcomes a loyal local crowd as well as international travellers from all over the world.

The dishes featured here emphasise simple, rustic cooking at its best. "Fine ingredients generally look after themselves" explains William, and "making these tasty dishes at home will bring amazing tastes and textures into the heart of your own home".

The Monro has been featured on television and is a favourite of the Sunday Press

SCOTTISH SMOKED SALMON AND MASCARPONE CREAM CHEESE ROULADE

SERVES 4

🍷 *Gewürztraminer Vin D'Alsace*

Method

Place a sheet of clingfilm on an oil based surface. To prevent movement, place salmon on clingfilm overlapping each piece. In a mixing bowl, add the cream cheese and chopped chives. Finally add the chopped shallots, a pinch of salt, pepper and lemon juice.

Stir continuously for 30 seconds then spoon the mixture onto smoked salmon carefully.

Then pinch both ends of clingfilm and fold. Leave in fridge for 45 minutes at 1°C.

When serving, place the pink tip spinach on to the serving plate. Remove the roulade from the fridge, take away clingfilm and slice with a sharp knife.

To serve

Assemble as in picture.

Ingredients

600g Scottish smoked salmon
300g Italian mascarpone cream cheese
2 banana shallots (chopped)
100g chives (chopped)
40g baby pink tip spinach
pinch of salt and cracked black pepper
juice from half a lemon

PAN ROASTED LOIN OF PORK ON CARROT SWEDE AND SMOKED BACON ROSTI POTATO WITH WILD MUSHROOMS AND RED WINE SAUCE

SERVES 4

 Pinot Noir

Ingredients

4 x 225g pork loin steaks
120g streaky bacon
200g wild mushrooms
250ml red wine
500ml good quality veal or beef stock

Rosti

4 carrots
2 swede (small)
80g smoked bacon

Method

For the sauce

First, reduce red wine in a saucepan by one third. Then, add veal or beef stock and simmer.

For the pork

Wrap the streaky bacon around the pork steaks using cocktail sticks to keep the bacon intact. Heat a frying pan and heat the pork on both sides and place in a hot oven at 200°C for 12 minutes. When the pork is ready, leave to rest for 3 minutes before serving.

For the mushrooms

In a separate pan, saute wild mushrooms and check seasoning. Add some of the chopped tarragon. Take off the heat when the mushrooms are tender but still firm.

For the rosti potato

Grate carrots and swede and add to chopped smoked bacon. Mix this with one egg. Season and mould into a shape and cook in a hot oven at 180°C for 10 minutes.

To serve

Present rosti onto a serving plate. Top with pork and place wild mushrooms around the plate. Complete the dish by simply pouring over the reduced red wine sauce.

RASPBERRY MASCARPONE AND WHITE CHOCOLATE CHEESECAKE

SERVES 4

🍷 *Codorniu Pinot Noir*
Brut Rose Cava

Ingredients

50g unsalted butter
225g ginger nut biscuits (crushed)

Filling

275g mascarpone cheese
2 eggs (beaten)
4tsp caster sugar
250g white chocolate
225g fresh raspberries

Topping

115g mascarpone cheese
75g fromage frais
white chocolate curls and raspberries to
decorate

Method

Preheat the oven to150°C/gas mark 2.

For the base

Melt the butter in a saucepan and stir in the crushed biscuits. Press into the base of a 9 inch springform cake tin.

For the filling

Beat the mascarpone and fromage frais in a bowl, then add the beaten egg and caster sugar, until evenly mixed.

Melt the white chocolate over hot water then stir into the cheese mixture with the fresh raspberries.

Spread evenly into the prepared tin, then bake for an hour until set.

Switch off the oven but do not remove the cheesecake, leave until cold.

Remove from the cake tin and place on a serving plate.

Make the topping by mixing the mascarpone and fromage frais, finish by spreading the mixture over the top of the cheesecake.

To serve

Decorate with the white chocolate curls and raspberries and serve.

160
PARKERS ARMS

Newton-in-Bowland, Nr Clitheroe, Lancashire BB7 3DY

01200 446 236
www.parkersarms.co.uk

Nestled in the rolling hills of the Trough of Bowland, in the beautiful village of Newton, you'll find The Parkers Arms, an imposing Georgian country-style inn where food provenance lies at the heart of everything.

Co-owned by Stosie Madi and Kathy Smith who have over 20 years experience as restaurateurs, the Parkers Arms is their fifth venture together and has built an enviable reputation with food aficionados across the North West.

As a French chef, seasonality and regionality means a great deal to Stosie, and this ethos ensures they only use the very best ingredients, sourced from Lancashire's finest artisan producers or foraged personally by Stosie herself.

Customers can enjoy a culinary journey through Stosie's ever evolving, seasonal and daily changing menus and signature dishes, including rustic hand-raised pies, potted Dunsop Bridge trout, cured Lune salmon and Bowland eggs to celebrate the 'terroir' of the Trough of Bowland.

Kathy's pastry genius contributes signature award winning puddings including the famous Wet Nelly and the mouth watering Chocolate Peanut Butter cheesecake.

Customers are charmed by the Parkers' chic and simple décor; its elegant dining room, roaring fires, its well appointed en-suite bedrooms and the panoramic views from the south facing garden.

Front of house is the realm of general manager AJ, who is ably assisted by a team of staff whose sole purpose is to ensure a warm welcome and an unfussy yet attentive service making a dining and drinking experience that is second to none.

Image by Jeff Singleton

Image by Chris Barber

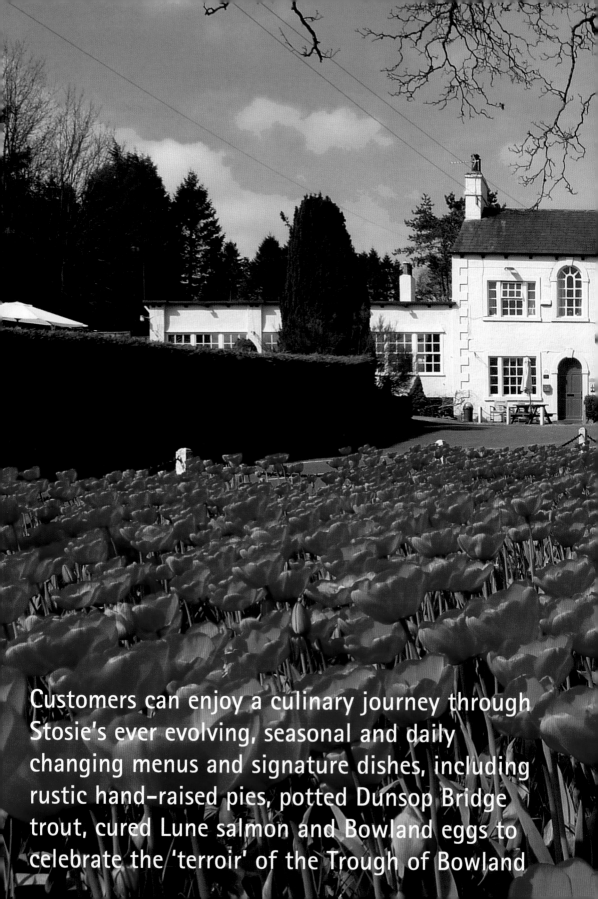

Customers can enjoy a culinary journey through Stosie's ever evolving, seasonal and daily changing menus and signature dishes, including rustic hand-raised pies, potted Dunsop Bridge trout, cured Lune salmon and Bowland eggs to celebrate the 'terroir' of the Trough of Bowland

SPICED POTTED DUNSOP BRIDGE TROUT, LEMON JELLY, BEER BREAD

SERVES 6

Finca de Arantei Alberino,
Spain 2008

Ingredients

6 small jars or 1 large jar

6 small fillets of very good quality, lightly smoked river trout (we use Dunsop Bridge Trout)

250g local unsalted butter cut into cubes (we use Caron Lodge)

1tsp each of mustard powder, fresh ground ginger, cayenne and nutmeg

4 cloves of garlic (peeled and the core removed)

3 large unwaxed lemons

1 large handful of flat leaf parsley

1 loaf of good country bread (sliced thick and toasted)

1 handful watercress

Method

Our rivers are full of delicious trout which we use all year round. River fish is by far more "terroir" in our immediate area in the trough of Bowland and although we use Sea fish we mainly celebrate wet and smoked river fish at Parkers.

For the garlic and lemon

Boil 250ml water in a small pan. As soon as it reaches a rolling boil blanch the garlic cloves for 1 minute, then drain and refresh the garlic in cold water. Repeat the process 5 times. Then using a pestle and mortar or hand blender, puree the garlic along with a level tablespoon of salt.

Grate the rind of all 3 lemons, then juice, sieve and reserve.

Pick the parsley leaves off the stalks and chop as finely as you can. Then put them aside.

For the potted trout

Peel the skins off the trout and flake the fish into large, rough flakes. Pick any bones out and discard them. Keep the skins.

Add the cubed butter to a heavy-based pan and place on a moderate heat. Bring to a boil and cook until the solids are brown and the oil is clear.

Allow to cool and sieve off the solids. Pour back the clarified butter into a clean pan and warm lightly. Add the trout skins and simmer for 2 minutes to infuse the smoked fish flavours, then remove skins and discard. Add all the dry spices and simmer for 2 minutes to release the oils. Keep warm.

In a bowl, mix the flaked fish with the garlic puree, the chopped parsley and the lemon rind, stir in the lemon juice then check the seasoning and pour into sterilised individual jars or 1 large kilner jar. Now pour on the warm, clarified butter and allow it to infuse for at least 24 hrs before eating.

To serve

Enjoy on slices of good toast and dip into the aromatic spiced butter. This will store for up to 3 months as long as the fish is preserved under the butter.

At the parkers we serve it with lemon jelly and handfuls of dressed watercress.

HAND RAISED BOWLAND VENISON PIE, PILLING SAMPHIRE, CREAMED MASH, BOWLAND ALE GRAVY

SERVES 6

Chateau Mayne Vieil Fronsac France 2005 or
Homemade Sloe Gin

Ingredients

Filling

500g minced venison
250g good quality, outdoor reared, local pork
from your butchers
100g good quality unsmoked streaky bacon
200ml local ale with 2tps redcurrant jelly
(reduced to half its original volume)
1 handful each of thyme, rosemary, parsley and
sage (chopped in a food processor with 100g of
lard (optional) to a smooth paste)
salt and pepper to taste

For the pastry

500g of good short crust pastry
or try your hand at making ours
400g plain flour
3 large eggs
125g softened butter
1tsp sugar
2tsp salt

Method

At Parkers we celebrate seasonality and locality and being in the Trough of Bowland means an abundance of game from local shoots. Pies at Parkers reflect "terroir" of the Lancashire region, our menu would be naked without our hand raised pies. Rustic robust characters "of the land" and very much contemporary country inn.

For the filling

Mix everything up in a bowl and leave to marinade 24hrs. The next day, season well with salt and pepper to taste and fry a little of the mixture to test the seasoning. Correct if necessary.

For the pastry

In a bowl or food processor mix all three dry ingredients well. Add the softened butter and mix thoroughly, add the eggs and bring the pastry together. If it is too dry, wet your hands and bring the pastry together. If a little wet and sticky dip your hands in flour first. Allow pastry to rest for 20 minutes in the fridge before rolling out as thin as you dare! Roll out individual pies if you wish or for a family of 6 roll half the pastry and place into a well greased tin. Press the filling in well then roll the rest of the pastry and cover the pie. Use a knife to form the edges. Glaze with a beaten egg and some milk, make a small hole in the centre and cook in a 180°C preheated oven for 35 minutes until golden.

To serve

Serve with creamed mash and seasonal vegetables. Samphire is delicious as the iodine salty taste complements the sweetness of the venison. This dish is also delicious the day after with piccalilli (a great alternative to pork pie).

KATHY'S AWARD WINNING WET NELLY, CUSTARD AND WHIPPED CREAM

SERVES 8

Domaine Grange Neuve Monbazillac, France 2007

Ingredients

Pastry

250g good sweet short crust pastry or try your hand at making ours
375g flour, 250g sugar
125g butter
1 egg
1tsp vanilla, 1tsp salt

Filling

(We make our own candied fruit but you can buy good quality candied fruit and peel)
50g candied orange, lime and lemon peel
50g candied ginger, cherries and chopped dates
50ml orange juice
50ml elderflower cordial
(preferably homemade or bottle bought if easier)
25g mixed spices (ginger, star anise, cinnamon, and nutmeg)
25g rind of unwaxed lemon, lime and orange peel (freshly grated)
100g cooked scones crumbled
100g jumbo oat flakes
100 fresh brown breadcrumbs

Method

Winner of best dessert pastry NWFF 2008.

Wet Nelly is a traditional pudding that is said to have originated in Liverpool and was named after Lord Nelson (wet because he was a seafarer and Nelly as in Nelson). Here at Parkers it is contemporised with the use of delicious ingredients. It is by far our best seller.

For the pastry

Mix the dry ingredients together by hand or using a food processor until it resembles fine breadcrumbs. Then add the butter, egg and vanilla to form a paste. Refrigerate.

Line a 28cm/11 inch loose-bottomed flan tin. Roll the pastry as thin as you dare and bake blind in a 180°C oven for 18 minutes until golden.

Remove tart case, brush the hot base with beaten egg yolk and return to oven for another 3 minutes.

For the filling

Allow 48 hours to prepare. Mix all the ingredients and leave to macerate overnight. Then add the cooked scone crumbs, jumbo oat flakes, brown breadcrumbs and a teaspoon of salt.

Mix the filling well and pour into the cooled tart case. Sprinkle with oats and brown sugar. Bake at 180°C for 35 minutes until set.

To serve

Serve warm with custard and ice cream.

170
PENINSULA DINING ROOM

3 Grosvenor Road, New Brighton CH45 2LW

0151 639 8338
www.peninsula-dining-room.co.uk

Peninsula dining room is situated on the Wirral peninsula in the seaside resort of New Brighton, having been open since June 2009 and now winning an army of admirers from all over the Wirral and beyond with its eclectic, yet value for money, uncomplicated food.

Chef / Patron Ross Gray and his Sous Chef Kane Dickinson have won several awards and achievements, most noticeably their inclusion in the Good Food Guide 2011 after only 16 months of being open.

With regular, changing menus every 8 weeks there is always something for everyone, including fantastic vegetarian and gluten free dishes.

PDR often hold gourmet nights and special evenings where menus are matched with wine offerings.

What with using only food from the UK, a certain amount of "greenness" comes into the restaurant with the team believing in the value as few food miles as possible.

Everything being made in house, from the breads to the ice cream, means mostly anything can be adapted and changed to the guests needs.

With Mandie Hickson running the floor the guests are well catered for by her and her excellent team.

The emphasis is always on simple yet flavoursome food and seems to be why this is one of the best and most popular restaurants on the Wirral.

Chef / Patron Ross Gray and his Sous Chef Kane Dickinson have won several awards and achievements most noticeably their inclusion in the Good Food Guide 2011 after only 16 months of being open

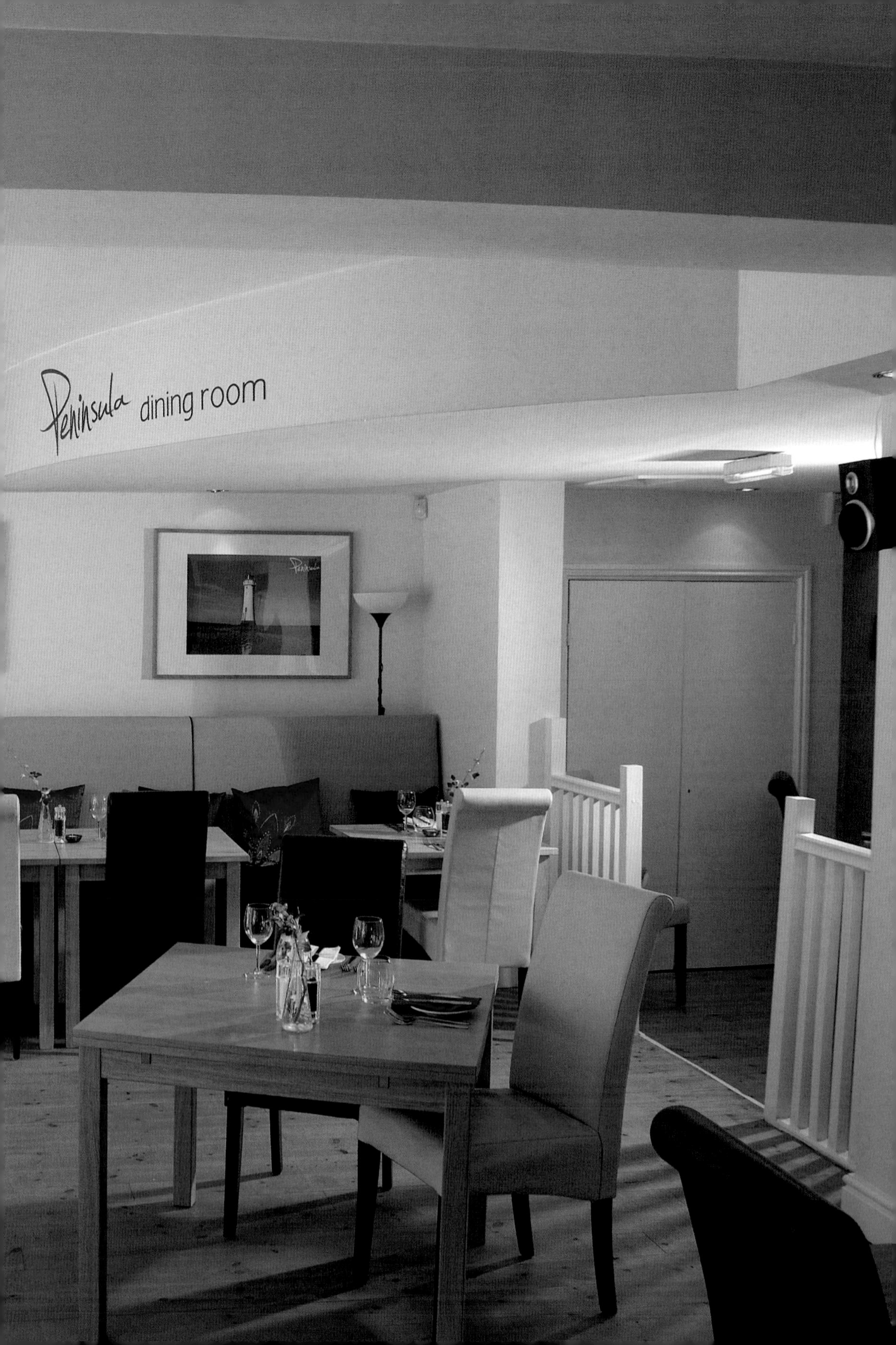
Peninsula dining room

HAM, CHEESE, PICKLE

SERVES 6-8

Las Manitos Viognier

Method

Cover the ham hocks with cold water and place a tight fitting lid or tightly wrap with tinfoil. Bring the ham hocks to the boil from cold and then turn down and simmer for 3 hours.

Leave to cool overnight in the liquid and when cool store in fridge.

Grate the cheddar and place to one side.

Take the ham hocks out, pick off the meat and place into a clean bowl. When you have picked it all, go through and shred it, checking for any gristle. Shred the meat until fine. Add the cheese and rough chopped parsley, add some of the jelly from the cooking liquor till it is just enough to combine.

Take out some clingfilm, place a large handful in centre and roll like a sausage. Hold either end of the clingfilm tightly and roll, then when tight tie each end. Chill for at least 6 hours.

For the mustard and pickle

Combine the mustard and mayonnaise and put in a squeezy bottle or keep in another type of container.

To serve

Drain your pickled vegetables on a J cloth and plate up as in the picture.

Ingredients

2 ham hocks
200g good strong cheddar (24 month aged Nicholas Barber cheddar)
small bunch flat parsley
1 tbsp English mustard
2 tbsp mayonnaise
pickled vegetables

SHIN OF BEEF

SERVES 6-8

 *Chateau Gasquerie*

Ingredients

1 kg beef shin
handful seasoned flour
200g smoked bacon (shredded)
600g carrots (diced)
300g onions (diced)
300g celery (diced)
½ bottle red wine
1 pint beef stock
4 tins tomatoes (chopped)

Blue Cheese Mascarpone

100g blue cheese (Grated, Blacksticks is the perfect cheese to use)
150g mascarpone

Method

For the beef shin

Dice the shin, wash in cold water and drain in colander. Sprinkle with seasoned flour. Heat up a frying pan with oil and quickly fry the meat. Once browned, put into a casserole dish. Fry off the bacon and add the diced vegetables. Once the diced vegetables are browned, add to the meat.

Add wine to the pan and de-glaze and add to the casserole dish. Add the tomatoes and slowly bring to the boil then add red wine and the stock.

Once the casserole is brought to the boil put a tight fitting lid on and place in a pre-heated, fan-assisted oven at 140°C for approximately 2½ hours. When it's cooked take it out and check the seasoning. Leave to cool for 10 minutes before serving.

For the blue cheese mascarpone

Add the cheese and the mascarpone and fold together.

To serve

Plate the shin onto large bowls with a spoonful of blue cheese mascarpone. Serve with pickled red cabbage and crusty bread.

A great winter family meal that everyone can tuck into.

SPARKLING ELDERFLOWER JELLY AND ROSE SORBET

SERVES 4

Gran Feudo Moscatel
Bodeags Chivite

Ingredients

Elderflower Jelly

400ml elderflower champagne
160ml sparkling wine
4 gelatine leaves

Rose Sorbet

(makes 6 – 8 scoops)
350ml natural yogurt
200g stock syrup (see below)
1 tbsp rose water
3 drops red food colouring

Stock Syrup

(This makes enough for 3 batches of ice cream
or sorbet)
200g caster sugar
200g liquid glucose
200ml water

Method

For the elderflower jelly

Heat the sparkling wine to 70°C.

Soak the gelatine in cold water for 5 minutes, then squeeze the gelatine out and dissolve in the sparkling wine. Cool to 37°C. Pour the sparkling wine and gelatine into the elderflower champagne and gently mix so that you don't lose the fizz.

Pour into 140ml moulds (pudding basins are ideal) and chill in the fridge.

For the stock syrup

Place all the ingredients in a pan and bring to the boil. Take off and leave to cool.

For the rose sorbet

Mix well and churn in an ice cream maker according to the manufacturer's instructions. At the restaurant we churn it for approximately 25-30 minutes.

To serve

Dip a mould in hot water for 5 seconds, drain excess liquid and place onto plate. They will keep their fizz for up to 48 hours. Serve with the rose sorbet as in picture.

180
PUSCHKA

16 Rodney Street, Liverpool L1 2TE

0151 708 8698
www.puschka.co.uk

Glen and Doug greeted their first guests to Puschka in 2001 and have built an unrivalled reputation ever since. The simple, honest, locally-sourced food, served fresh from their little kitchen to the highest possible standard. The attentive and friendly service is all served up in an environment that once sampled is impossible to forget.

Nestling in Liverpool's old Georgian Quarter, Puschka's French oak panelling and signature pink walls proudly display artwork from local artists and has in turn been described as a 'funky, bohemian restaurant' and as a 'hidden gem'. In a slow baked, perfectly seasoned nutshell, this is what they are all about.

Firm favourites like potted Southport shrimps with sweet crab claw, or balsamic red onion and rosemary marinated lamb rump, provide regulars and newcomers with a comforting taste of home, while the ever changing specials board gives the menu a seasonal facelift.

With top secret Pop-Up events happening all over the North West, a thriving outside catering business that delivers 'Fresh Food Fast' to the discerning festival goer and a brand new daytime menu, it looks like another ten successful years will be a breeze.

As Glen says, "We love cooking, we love eating and more importantly we love the way that food and wine brings friends and family together. A communion of sorts creates a good time for sure."

Nestling in Liverpool's old Georgian Quarter, Puschka's French oak panelled and signature pink walls proudly display artwork from local artists and has in turn been described as a 'funky, bohemian restaurant' and as a 'hidden gem'. In a slow baked, perfectly seasoned nutshell, this is what they are all about

BALLOTINE OF CHICKEN, TARRAGON AND BABY LEEKS, PUY LENTIL VINAIGRETTE

SERVES 4

🍷 *Gavi di Gavi La Meirana,*
Bruno Broglia

Ingredients

Ballotine

2 large, skinless chicken breasts
2 egg yolks
25ml double cream
2 tbsp fresh tarragon (chopped)
2 tbsp wholegrain mustard
cracked black pepper
Maldon sea salt
8 baby leeks (blanched)

Vinaigrette

200g puy lentils
1 pint of stock
125ml extra virgin olive oil
25ml white wine vinegar
1 tbsp Dijon mustard
2 cloves of garlic
salt and pepper
parsley (chopped)

Method

For the chicken ballotine

Blend all the ingredients in a food processer until smooth.
Trim the leeks and plunge them into boiling, salted water for 3 minutes. Then remove and refresh in iced water.

Roll out two 12" double layers of clingfilm and place the chicken mixture in a rectangle in the centre, then place the leeks across the length of the mixture in the middle. Roll the mixture in the clingfilm into a sausage shape and seal the ends like a Christmas cracker. Place into boiling water, cover and simmer for 20 to 25 minutes. Remove and allow to cool overnight.

For the puy lentil vinaigrette

Boil puy lentils in stock for 20 minutes until tender. Drain and cool. Blend Dijon mustard, garlic and white wine vinegar. Gradually add olive oil then add cooled lentils and parsley, season to taste.

To serve

Assemble as in the picture.

RUMP OF LAMB, BALSAMIC, ROSEMARY & RED ONION MARINADE, ROASTED GARLIC MASH, GREEN BEANS

SERVES 4

Coteaux Du Tricastin,
Rhone

Ingredients

4 x 225g lamb rumps
4 cloves garlic (chopped)
4 tbsp rosemary (chopped)
1 large red onion (thinly sliced)
2 tbsp soft brown sugar
100ml balsamic vinegar

4 large Maris Peer potatoes
125ml double cream
50g salted butter
1 whole garlic bulb
200g green beans (trimmed)

Method

Preheat oven to 225°C.

To prepare the lamb

Score the lamb skin and place in marinade, coating all sides. Leave in the fridge for at least 24hrs.

For the potatoes

Boil the potatoes in salted water until tender, then dry out and mash. Heat butter and cream until the butter melts and gradually add to the mash, season to taste. Wrap garlic bulb in tin foil and bake for 30 minutes. Squeeze garlic paste into the mash to taste.

For the lamb

Sear lamb rumps in a very hot non stick pan on all sides till browned. Place in the oven for 10-12 minutes. Allow to rest for 5 minutes before serving.

Cook trimmed beans in boiling water for 2 to 3 minutes.

To serve

Assemble as in picture with a sprig of rosemary.

TREACLE TART, ORANGE ZEST ICE CREAM

SERVES 4

🍷 *Muscat Beaumes de Venise,*
Pierre Perrin

Method

For the pastry

Pulse pastry mix until it forms into a ball. Wrap in clingfilm and chill in the fridge for an hour.

For the filling

Gently warm all the ingredients in a heavy bottomed pan until combined. Line a flan dish with pastry, pour in the filling and bake for 30 minutes at 200°C. The treacle filling should be set but not too firm.

For the orange ice cream

Simmer the zest, juice, sugar and water. Then reduce by half in a heavy bottomed pan and allow to cool. Lightly whisk the egg whites to soft peaks and fold into the cool syrup and the cream and churn in an ice cream maker.

To serve

Assemble as in picture.

Ingredients

Pastry

300g plain flour
260g butter cubes (chilled)
2 tbsp water (chilled)

Filling

780g golden syrup
225g white breadcrumbs
2 whole lemons (zest and juice)

Orange Ice Cream

zest and juice of 3 oranges
170g caster sugar
2 egg whites
300ml double cream
150ml cold water

0151 932 0937
www.rhubarbandcustard.net

Rhubarb and Custard's slogan 'Good food will reign supreme', represents the ethos surrounding this rapidly growing catering company!
The concept of Rhubarb and Custard was founded by Steven Burgess, 25, after his experiences as a chef in many top restaurants. Sourcing all their fresh produce, locally, from reputable suppliers, Steven and his team provide the highest class and quality of food and service to customers' homes and at all kinds of events. Rhubarb and Custard is one of Liverpool's finest specialised outside catering companies with a difference.

Using a team of professionally trained chefs, they deliver excellent results and a personalised service at a whole range of events including buffets, corporate entertaining, dinner parties, bowl food and banqueting. Their menus are varied and bespoke, using locally sourced, fresh ingredients, specifically designed to stand out from the crowd with modern twists, classic combinations and firm favourites guaranteed to make your party memorable.

And there's more! 'Rhubarb At Home', offers a hands-on cookery course programme available at your house or at their premises in Crosby. The three hour course ranges from 'couldn't boil an egg' to vegetarian, French bistro, dinner party favourites and healthy foods.

Their cookery programme for children and parents, to educate them on how to cook fresh healthy food, in partnership with the local schools in Crosby, is another element that is extremely popular.

Rhubarb and Custard's emphasis towards great food is "less is more". They believe in a simple approach towards cooking that produces finer results and more of the true taste of an ingredient rather than masking the beauty of it. The concept of creating a wonderful bespoke menu, using freshly sourced local ingredients, just as a top Merseyside or Lancashire restaurant would, is brought directly to the customers' door.

The concept of Rhubarb and Custard was founded by Steve Burgess, 25, after his experience as a chef in many top restaurants. Sourcing all their fresh produce, locally, from reputable suppliers, Steve and his team provide the highest class and quality of food and service to customers' homes and at all kinds of

CONFIT SALMON, PICKLED CUCUMBER, SALTED CAULIFLOWER, ORANGE, RADISH, SHALLOT

SERVES 4

Bolney Wine Estate Pinot Grigio, 2010

Ingredients

Salmon

4 salmon fillets (deboned and skinned)
500ml olive oil

Cucumber Pickle

½ cucumber (peeled into ribbons)
100ml white wine vinegar
75g caster sugar
1 stick of cinnamon
½ vanilla pod (scraped and deseeded)

Salted Cauliflower

1 baby cauliflower
75g Maldon sea salt

Garnish

banana shallots (thinly sliced)
radishes (thinly sliced)
segmented orange slices
borage leaves
baby red vein sorrel

Method

For the salmon

Put the olive oil in a pan large enough to hold the 4 salmon fillets and bring the oil up to 55°C on a low heat. Place the salmon in the pan and cook for 15 minutes, then remove with a slotted spoon and drain. Flake the fish ready to serve.

For the pickled cucumber

Warm the white wine vinegar, sugar and spices until the sugar has dissolved. Drop the cucumber ribbons into this mixture and take off the heat.

For the cauliflower

Pick the cauliflower down into individual florets and put them into a sieve with a bowl underneath. Generously sprinkle the sea salt over the cauliflower and leave to stand in the fridge overnight.

To serve

Drain the cucumber ribbons of any pickle liquor, lay them on a plate and place the salmon on top of the ribbons. Wash the cauliflower thoroughly under cold water and decorate the plate with the cauliflower florets, radishes, oranges shallots and leaves.

ROASTED PORK BELLY, PRESSED APPLE AND RAISINS, SPICED CARROT PUREE, BALSAMIC SHALLOTS, PISTACHIO

SERVES 4

 Chianti Riserva 2006/2007
Villa Dante

Ingredients

Pork Belly

2kg whole pork belly
2 carrots (peeled)
2 sticks celery
4 bay leaves
1 head garlic
1 bunch thyme
1 white onion
bottle of Magner's cider
½ bottle of white wine

Apple and Raisins

10 Granny Smith apples
small handful of raisins
100ml Madeira
100g unsalted butter (melted)
50g demerara sugar
4 tsp ground cinnamon
25ml honey

Spiced Carrot Puree

2 carrots (peeled, chopped and boiled until tender)
2 tbsp butter
4 tsp olive oil
salt and pepper
1 tsp ground cumin

Shallots

400g shallots (peeled)
50g butter
2 tbsp olive oil
4 tbsp balsamic vinegar

Garnish

fresh apple (cut into matchsticks)
pistachios (crushed)

Method

For the pork belly

Chop all the vegetables and lay them in a deep tray, placing the belly pork on top. Then pour the alcohol all over the pork and vegetables.

Cover the tin with tin foil and cook on 220°C for 4 hours until very tender.

Once cooked, place the pork between two sheets of greaseproof paper and between two baking trays. Press down on the top tray with weights and leave overnight.

For the pressed apples

Marinate the raisins in Madeira for 2/3 days before cooking.

Core the apples then slice them as thinly as possible using a mandolin.

Start laying apples out in a small baking tray lined with greaseproof paper. After each layer, brush with melted butter and sprinkle with sugar, raisins and cinnamon. Repeat until all the ingredients are used up.

Once the top of the tray has been reached, place a buttered piece of greaseproof on top then cook in a preheated oven at 160°C for 40 minutes until tender.

Place another baking tray on top and press overnight.

For the carrot puree

Place cooked carrots in a blender with butter and olive oil, seasoning with a little cumin, salt and pepper.

Blend until smooth.

For the shallots

Sweat the shallots off slowly in a pan with oil for as long as possible without them overcooking. Add butter and balsamic vinegar then turn up the heat. Reduce until slightly sticky.

To serve

Cut the belly pork to the required size then pan-fry skin side down. Once the skin has started to crackle, turn it over and place in preheated oven at 180°C.

Cut the terrine into the desired shape and glaze with honey. Then put it into the oven along with the pork belly.

Swipe the carrot puree across the plate and place the glazed terrine on the puree, then place the pork belly on the terrine.

Garnish with apples and pistachios.

STRAWBERRY & VANILLA CRUMBLE, CLOTTED CREAM CUSTARD

SERVES 4

🍷 *Laurent-Perrier Cuvée Rosé
NV Champagne*

Ingredients

Strawberries

30/32 large strawberries
1 vanilla pod
juice of ½ lemon
30g caster sugar

Crumble

50g flaked almonds
200g self-raising flour
140g brown or white sugar
125g cold butter (cubed)

Custard

250ml double cream
250ml whole milk
3 egg yolks
100g sugar
100g clotted cream

Method

For the strawberries

Put all the ingredients into a saucepan and bring them up to a low heat for 15 minutes, stirring now and again.

Once the juice has started to come out of the strawberries and make a syrup, take them off the heat.

For the crumble

Mix the butter and flour with your fingers until it has a breadcrumb texture, and then fold in the almond and sugar.

Place the crumble mix onto a baking tray and bake at 160°C, turning every 5 minutes until golden.

For the custard

Warm up milk and cream, then separately whisk the eggs and sugar together until light and fluffy.

Pour the milk and cream onto the eggs and sugar and return the mixture to the heat. Then whisk in the clotted cream.

Cook out until the mixture has a thick consistency.

To serve

Place strawberries at the bottom of individual serving dishes and sprinkle the crumble on top.

Then pour custard into a serving jug and garnish with strawberries.

200
SALT HOUSE TAPAS

Salt House, Hanover Street L1 3DW

0151 706 0092
www.salthousetapas.co.uk

Situated opposite John Lewis in Liverpool's vibrant L1 in an historic former bishop's residence, Salt House Tapas has quickly gained a reputation in the city for its quality and friendliness.

Independently owned and run, the restaurant is building its reputation of being one of the few places where the owners cook the food, pour the drinks and clear the tables. Martin Renshaw, the Executive Chef/Partner, has left a globetrotting career to return to Merseyside. With a compelling passion for quality he has helped to alter people's perception of the old-fashioned view of tapas. Using the best Spanish produce from Iberico hams, padron peppers and cheeses to the best olives you'll ever taste, each tapas dish is a little piece of perfection.

The menu changes with the seasons and there are daily specials on the chalkboard making the most of the local supplier's fantastic produce. Come in for a fabulous dinner with friends, an ice cold Spanish beer on a sunny day or just a coffee and a chat.

The menu changes with the seasons and there are daily specials on the chalkboard, making the most of the local supplier's fantastic produce. Come in for a fabulous dinner with friends, an ice cold Spanish beer on a sunny day, or just a coffee and a chat

SCALLOPS, SPICED LENTILS, PANCETTA, WILTED SPINACH

SERVES 4

🍷 *Martin Codax, Rias Biaxas, Spain 2008, Albarino*

Method

For the spiced lentils

Blanch the lentils in unsalted water until tender and refresh. Finely dice the shallots and the piquillo peppers. Saute the pancetta until evenly browned and crisp.

Saute the shallots in a little of the pancetta fat then add the peppers, and paprika cook for 1 minute.

Add the lentils, vinegar, lemon juice and zest then toss together. Heat a non-stick pan with a little pomace oil until smoking and then season the scallops with Maldon salt flakes.

For the scallops

Sear the scallops for 1½ minutes each side depending on size. Place three dessert spoons of lentils on a rectangular plate and top with three scallops per serving.

To serve

Dust with coral powder, top with pea shoots, drizzle with virgin oil.

Ingredients

Scallops

12 Scallops

Spiced Lentils

200g puy lentils
16 (4 each) piquillo peppers
8 (2 each) shallots
1 dsp Moscatel vinegar
1 tsp paprika dulce
2 lemons (juice and zest)
100g pancetta lardons
pomace oil
maldon salt flakes for seasoning

PORK CHEEKS, MORCILLA CANNELLINI BEANS

SERVES 6

🍷 *Papa Luna, Calatayud, Spain 2007, Garnacha/Shiraz*

Ingredients

6 pork cheeks
8 sprigs of rosemary
1 garlic bulb (crushed)
1 shallot
1 carrot
2 celery sticks
1 leek
80g tomato puree
2 bay leaves
1 dsp black peppercorns (crushed)
50ml red wine
100ml rosemary infused virgin oil
250g cannellini beans
4 dps tomato concasse
2 dsp parsley
4 morcilla sliced in half
4 dsp caramelised onions

Method

Dice all the veg into 1cm cubes.

Heat the pomace oil in a large saute pan. Fry the pork cheeks until golden brown, place into a roasting tray.

Then add and fry all the veg until browned, add the puree and a little wine.

Reduce until the puree begins to caramelise, then add the rest of the wine in stages and continue to reduce.

Add the reduction to the pork cheeks, then add the peppercorns, bay leaves and rosemary. Add enough brown chicken stock to cover the cheeks. Braise on gas mark 2 for 3½ hours.

Remove the cheeks and pass the sauce, use the sauce to reheat the cheeks when serving. Warm the virgin oil with the beans for 3 to 4 minutes over a medium heat, crush lightly with a fork.

Add the concasse, caramelised onions and the parsley, stir and season. Sear the morcilla on one side for 2 minutes, turn and place under salamander (the grill) for 2 minutes more.

To serve

Serve a cheek on top of the beans with morcilla to one side. Garnish with beer battered shallots.

DARK CHOCOLATE ALMOND TORTE

SERVES 12

🍷 *Pedro Ximinez 'Antique' Fernando de Castilla, Spain*

Method

For the crème fraiche

It is best to start the day before by making the cardomon infused crème fraiche. First bring the sugar and water to the boil. Next, crush the cardomon pods and add them to this syrup. Then remove it from the heat and pour it into a clean container, leaving it to infuse overnight. In the morning pass the syrup through a fine sieve, and add about a third of it to the crème fraiche. The rest can be reserved for later.

For the torte

Start by preheating the oven to 150°C and also greasing and lining a cake tin. Melt the chocolate over a bain-marie and, while it is cooling pulse the almonds in a food processor until roughly chopped.

Cream together the butter and sugar until it is light and pale then beat in the egg yolks, one at a time, incorporating well after each yolk is added. Then fold in the chocolate and the almonds.

Take the egg whites and whisk them into soft peaks, then fold them into the chocolate mixture.

Pour this into the prepared cake tin and bake for 1 hour 10 minutes, or until firm.

To serve

Serve with cardamon infused crème fraiche.

Ingredients

Torte

25g dark chocolate pistols
25g almonds (whole and blanched)
25g butter (unsalted, room temperature)
8 eggs (separated)

Cardomon Infused Crème Fraiche

100ml water
15g caster sugar
8 cardomon pods
200g crème fraiche

210
THE SIDE DOOR

29a Hope Street, Liverpool L1 9BQ

0151 707 7888
www.thesidedoor.co.uk

The culinary institution that is the highly acclaimed Side Door Restaurant is in the heart of Liverpool's most important conservation area; the Georgian Hope Street Quarter, alongside the Philharmonic Hall and in between the Cathedrals. It is ideally placed for theatre and concert goers. Run by Sheila and Sean who have a reputation for serving delicious, freshly prepared, imaginative and seasonal dishes to regulars and visitors alike.

Their menus change weekly and the specials daily, using locally sourced produce. Diners are likely to enjoy fish landed that very morning at Fleetwood, with fresh vegetables from Cheshire and Lancashire.

Chef Sean Millar, who perfected his culinary skills at a top Zurich hotel, says the secret of the Side Door's success is its homely and welcoming atmosphere and the ever-changing seasonal menus.

Co-owner Sheila Benson and her front of house staff create an atmosphere that, whilst relaxed, is highly professional.

Says Sean: "I speak to suppliers every day to ensure we select the best available fish and meats. We like fish dishes because of our great relationship with our Fleetwood merchant who still trawls the North sea, and our ability to track down wild salmon or brown trout from fly fishers in Scotland. "

"On concert nights we know customers have to be in and out within 90 minutes, and it works perfectly. Nobody has ever been late for a concert! Many concert goers have been coming to us for years, and for us that speaks volumes."

Their menus change weekly and the specials daily, using locally sourced produce. Diners are likely to enjoy fish landed that very morning at Fleetwood, with fresh vegetables from Cheshire and Lancashire

GRILLED QUAIL WITH HOUMOUS AND HARISSA

SERVES 4

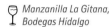

🍷 *Manzanilla La Gitana,*
Bodegas Hidalgo

Ingredients

4 quails (cut in half down the middle)

Harissa

2 red peppers (roasted, peeled and de-seeded)
4 red chillies (halved and de-seeded)
2 garlic cloves
1 dsp tomato puree
1 dsp white wine vinegar
1 tsp smoked paprika
4 tsp cumin seeds (ground)
4 tbsp olive oil

Houmous

200g dried chickpeas (soaked in water overnight)
6 tbsp olive oil
juice of 1 lemon
3 tbsp tahini paste
6 tbsp good olive oil
2 cloves garlic (mashed to a paste with a pinch of salt)

Method

For the harissa

Blend the chillies with the garlic until smooth, then add the remaining ingredients except the olive oil and blend again until smooth. At this stage, drizzle in the olive oil while the motor is still running and season to taste.

For the houmous

Rinse the chickpeas under cold water then place in a large saucepan and cover them with water. Bring them to the boil, then reduce the heat and simmer for about 1½ hours or until tender. When cooked, drain the chickpeas but retain a little of the cooking liquid. Blend the chickpeas in a food processor with a little of the cooking liquid until smooth, then add the lemon juice, garlic, tahini and the olive oil. Blend well and season to taste.

For the quail

Place the quail in a large mixing bowl and add 1 tbsp of the harissa paste with a drizzle of olive oil and mix together well. Skewer each quail (2 halves) and grill them under a hot grill for about 8 minutes. You could also grill them on a barbecue.

To serve

Divide the houmous between 4 plates and place a skewered quail on each. Then garnish with some fresh, chopped, flat leaf parsley, olives, a drizzle of olive oil, a pinch of smoked paprika and a little more harissa on top. We also add a few roasted whole almonds.

ROAST COD FILLET WITH SLOW COOKED FENNEL, DILL MASH AND SOUTHPORT SHRIMP BUTTER

SERVES 4

Matteo Correggia Roero Arneis Piedmont, 2009

Ingredients

4 x 200g cod fillets
100g Southport brown shrimps
75g butter

Slow Cooked Fennel

100ml olive oil
4 medium sized fennel bulbs (cut into quarters, core trimmed and green herbs kept aside)
100ml water
juice of half a lemon
sea salt and pepper

Dill Mash

1 kg peeled potatoes (we use either rooster or Cyprus)
3 cloves garlic
3 tbsp fresh dill (roughly chopped)
75g butter (melted)
enough milk and water to cover

Method

For the slow cooked fennel

Heat the oil in a large saucepan over a high heat and add the fennel with a little sea salt and black pepper. Cook for 5 minutes, turning each piece until golden and caramelised on both sides. Lower the heat and add the water and lemon juice, then cover with greaseproof paper. Simmer slowly for about 20 minutes until all the water has evaporated, then chop the fennel herbs and sprinkle over.

For the dill mash

Place the potatoes in a saucepan with the garlic and cover with half milk and half water. Bring to the boil and then reduce the heat and simmer for about 15 minutes, or until soft. Drain the potatoes, but reserve some of the cooking liquid. Mash the potatoes with the garlic and add some of the cooking liquid and melted butter until it reaches the consistency you prefer. Stir in the chopped dill and season to taste.

For the cod and shrimp

Place a frying pan with a heat resistant handle (large enough to hold your cod) over a high heat and add about 3 tablespoons of olive oil. Season the cod well and carefully place each piece, skin-side up, into the pan. Gently shake the pan to prevent the cod from sticking. Add a knob of butter and cook for about 2 minutes, then carefully turn the fish over and place in a preheated oven for about 8 minutes. You could also transfer the cod onto a roasting tray drizzled with a little olive oil if your frying pan handle isn't heat resistant!

Heat the butter with the shrimps and a squeeze of lemon juice until it just starts to brown and has that lovely nutty smell to it.

To serve

Divide the fennel between 4 warm serving plates and place a large spoonful of the dill mash next to them. Place each cod fillet on top of the mash and spoon over the shrimp butter.

RHUBARB AND CUSTARD TART

SERVES 10

🍷 *Chateau Le Fage, Monbazillac, France 2007*

Ingredients

Pastry Case

200g plain flour
100g butter
60g icing sugar
2 egg yolks

Rhubarb and Custard Filling

500g rhubarb
500ml water
400g caster sugar
1 vanilla pod (seeds scraped out)
600ml whipping cream
8 egg yolks

Method

For the pastry case

Either by hand or in a food processor, combine the flour, butter and sugar until you have a texture similar to breadcrumbs. Add the egg yolks and mix until all the ingredients come together. If it looks too dry, add a tiny splash of cream or milk. Then shape it into a ball, wrap it in clingfilm and leave to chill for about 45 minutes. After this, roll it out onto a floured surface to about 5mm thick and press into a 24cm tart tin. Prick the base with a sharp knife and chill for a further 30 minutes. Pre-heat your oven to 220°C/gas 7 and bake the tart shell for about 10 minutes or until light brown. Then allow to cool.

For the rhubarb and custard filling

Trim each end of the rhubarb and slice it into 6cm pieces. Bring the water and half the sugar to the boil and reduce by half. Add the rhubarb and simmer for about 3-5 minutes, or until just cooked, then remove the rhubarb and leave to cool. The syrup can be reserved for another time. Arrange the rhubarb in the pastry shell. Bring about 5 inches of water to the boil in a saucepan which should be smaller than the bowl you will be using for your custard mix. In a large, metal bowl, whisk the remaining sugar, egg yolks and vanilla seeds together for about 5 minutes until smooth. Bring the cream to the boil and whisk it into the egg mixture then set the bowl over the saucepan and whisk until it becomes thickened after about 8-10 minutes. Then lower the heat in the oven to 180°C/gas 4 and pour the custard mixture over the rhubarb. Bake for a further 40 minutes.

To serve

Assemble as in the picture.

SPIRE RESTAURANT

Number One, Church Road, Liverpool L15 9EA

0151 734 5040
www.spirerestaurant.co.uk

Recently crowned 'The Good Food Guide's North West Restaurant of the Year 2011', Spire has just celebrated its fifth birthday. Attracting nationwide custom, this cosy, gastronomic gem is the creation of Adam and Matt Locke; two friendly, unassuming South Liverpool brothers with stacks of skills and passion. They're committed to providing top quality fine dining but, crucially, in a relaxed, unpretentious atmosphere where Adam makes everyone feel individually welcome with his genuine warmth and geniality.

Spire's modern British and European menu brims with carefully considered dishes, skillfully executed, reflecting originality and savoir-faire. Chef Matt has an impressive list of credentials: he completed his professional training at St David's Hotel in North Wales with internships at Longueville Manor, Jersey, and The Greenhouse, London under Gary Rhodes. He went on to work at Edinburgh's Holly Rood Hotel where he cooked before the Queen and Prince Philip at private dinings, and also at the Craxton Wood Hotel and The London Carriage Works. Matt's cooking style harnesses creativity, precision and sheer food mastery. His sensitively structured flavour-texture combinations are often described as sublime. All this culinary genius is packed into a modest, unpretentious individual who rarely ventures from the kitchen to soak up the abundant praise that perpetually spills from his customers.

Spire is committed to supporting local producers and Adam nurtures close relationships with a handful of

excellent local suppliers of meat, fish, vegetables and cheese. Matt works with seasonal and responsibly sourced ingredients, shaping the menus to fit these criteria. Wine connoisseurs will be impressed with a comprehensive and widely respected wine list, the result of Adam's keen understanding of grape varieties, vintage and matching wine with food.

Specialising in modern British and European cuisine, Spire promises culinary expertise and a convivial ambience at one of the most popular and critically acclaimed eateries in the North West of England

DIVER SCALLOPS WITH BLACK PUDDING, CRISPY QUAIL'S EGGS, CAULIFLOWER PURÉE, RED WINE SAUCE

SERVES 4

🍷 *Peacock Ridge Sauvignon Blanc*

Ingredients

12 hand-dived scallops (removed from shells and cleaned)
2 slices Parma ham
2 Bury black puddings

Crispy Quail's Eggs

8 quail's eggs
flour
1 egg (beaten)
breadcrumbs

Cauliflower Purée

200g cauliflower
50g butter
75g cream
15ml water
salt and pepper

75ml freshly made red wine sauce

Method

For the cauliflower purée

Cut the cauliflower into small florets and place them into a large pan along with the butter, water and a pinch of salt. Cover the pan and sweat on a low temperature for about 20 minutes until the cauliflower is soft. Add the cream, then blend the cauliflower and pass the purée through a fine sieve into a bowl. Adjust the seasoning as required and set aside, keeping warm by covering with clingfilm.

For the black pudding and Parma ham

Slice the black pudding into 12 rounds of 5mm thickness.

Sandwich the ham between two sheets of greaseproof paper and place on a baking tray. Place another baking tray with a heavy weight on top. Bake in the oven on 160°C for 8-12 minutes until the ham is crispy.

For the quail's eggs

Bring a deep pan of water to the boil and add a little vinegar. Turn the quail's eggs upside down in their box so that the fat end faces upwards, then carefully cut the end off with a sharp, serrated knife. Poach the eggs one by one for about 10 -15 seconds each. Then plunge the cooked egg into an ice bath to halt cooking. Remove from the water and drain on a piece of clean kitchen paper.

Roll the cooled eggs in the flour, then the beaten egg, then the breadcrumbs. Repeat.

To assemble

In a non-stick frying pan, sauté the black pudding discs until slightly crisp on both sides. Set aside.

Bring a clean, non-stick pan to smoking point. Place the scallops flat-side down and cook for 1-2 minutes depending on size. When the scallops start to turn a golden caramel colour on top, turn them over. Add a knob of butter, season, and cook for a further minute or so until fully cooked.

Deep fry the quail's eggs in corn oil.

To serve

Drag a spoonful of the cauliflower purée across the plate. Place the 3 black pudding discs in a line, each topped with a scallop. Place 2 quail's eggs between the 3 scallops. Garnish with a few pieces of the baked Parma ham. Drizzle with red wine sauce.

RUMP OF SALT MARSH LAMB, PASTILLES OF VEGETABLES, LYONNAISE POTATOES WITH SHALLOT AND MINT CONFIT, CRISPY LAMB'S SHOULDER, LAMB JUS

SERVES 4

 Chateau de Balan

Ingredients

4 x 227g Lancashire Salt Marsh lamb rump

50g confit of lamb shoulder
pantzo breadcrumbs
1 egg
flour for dusting

Potatoes

200g ratte potatoes (washed and peeled)
garlic
thyme
2 tbsp olive oil

Shallot and Mint Confit

100g shallots
50g butter
olive oil
140ml red wine jus
10g mint

Vegetables

200g broad beans
2 large carrots (peeled and sliced into 3)
1 courgette (sliced into 3)
150g asparagus tips

100ml lamb jus

Method

For the lamb

Remove the outer skin from the rumps, leaving the creamy fat on show. Leave at room temperature for 30 minutes prior to cooking.

For the potatoes

Cut into 2.5cm thick slices and, using a small cutter (no bigger than a 10p piece), cut discs from the potato slices. You will need 3 discs per portion. Cover with a damp cloth.

For the shallot and mint confit

Peel and slice the shallots very thinly. Heat the butter and oil in a pan until foaming, add the shallots and cook on a low heat until soft and very slightly caramelised. Add red wine jus and season. Simmer until the sauce has reduced to a thick consistency. Add the finely chopped mint and check seasoning. Set aside to cool.

For the vegetables

Pick the broad beans and blanch briefly in boiling, salted water. Refresh in an ice bath, and remove skins. Using an apple corer, cut small barrel shaped pastilles from the carrots and courgette. Cook the carrots in salted, sugared water until al dente. Cook the asparagus tips and courgettes in boiling salted water for 1 and a half minutes, then put into an ice bath to retain colour.

For the confit of lamb

Finely dice the confit of lamb shoulder. Dust with flour, dip into the egg, then roll the dice in the pantzo breadcrumbs and set them aside. Now cook the lamb rump. Preheat the oven to 200°C, heat the olive oil in a pan and colour the lamb on all sides. Season and transfer to the oven for 8-10 minutes. Remove and leave to rest on a rack for 6-8 minutes.

To assemble

Pan-fry the potato discs in olive oil and butter until golden brown. Add garlic and thyme and place in the oven at 200°C for 5 minutes until the potatoes are soft. Take one of the discs and place a heaped spoonful of the shallot mix on top. Cover with a second disc and repeat, finishing with the third disc. Place the diced shoulder in a shallow fryer for 1 minute until brown and crispy. Drain on clean kitchen paper and sprinkle with salt.

To serve

Place a potato stack in the middle of a plate and surround with slender slices of the lamb. Reheat the vegetables in butter and water and arrange on the plate with the diced shoulder. Serve with the lamb jus.

SPICED, POACHED TARPORLEY RHUBARB IN GINGER CRUMBLE, WITH BLACKBERRY AND CLOVE JELLY, CUSTARD ICE CREAM

SERVES 4

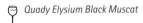 *Quady Elysium Black Muscat*

Ingredients

Poached Rhubarb

4 or 5 sticks of Tarporley rhubarb
570ml water
570g white caster sugar
2 star anise
1 cinnamon stick
5 black peppercorns
a thin slice of fresh ginger
juice of 1 lime
a thin slice of orange rind

Crumble

50g soft butter
80g plain flour
40g light muscovado sugar
35g rolled oats
⅛ to ¼ tsp ginger powder

Blackberry Jelly

350g frozen blackberries
150g sugar
2 cloves
100ml apple juice
3 leaves gelatin
1 cinnamon stick

homemade custard ice cream

Method

For the poached rhubarb

Place all the ingredients except the rhubarb into a pan and bring to the boil.

Remove from heat, cover and set aside for 1 hour for the flavours to infuse into the syrup. Wash and portion the rhubarb; place it in an ovenproof dish.

Sprinkle with a little sugar and cover with the infused syrup.

Cover the dish with tin foil or a lid and cook in the oven at 200°C for 10-15 minutes, until the rhubarb is soft but holds its shape.

Remove from the oven and set aside on a tray lined with greaseproof paper.

Strain the syrup and return half of it to a pan, gently reducing until it is quite sticky. Allow to cool.

For the crumble

Place all the ingredients together in a large bowl and rub them together between your fingers until they resemble fine breadcrumbs.

Spread this out onto a baking tray lined with greaseproof paper and cook in the oven at 180°C for about 20 minutes. Allow to cool and set aside.

For the blackberry jelly

Place the berries, sugar, cinnamon and cloves into a saucepan and heat gently. When the sugar has dissolved and the berries have softened, remove from heat and allow them to infuse for 20 minutes.

Soak the gelatin for 5 minutes. Add the apple juice to the berries, reheat and then pass through a fine sieve or muslin. While the strained liquid is still hot, whisk in the gelatin until completely dissolved. Pour into moulds and reserve in the fridge until set.

To serve

Dip the rhubarb in the cooled syrup and roll in the cooked crumble. Place the crumble-coated spiced rhubarb on a plate. Turn out a blackberry and clove jelly next to the rhubarb.

Serve with a scoop of homemade custard ice-cream.

AN INTRODUCTION FROM CLAIRE LARA, MASTERCHEF THE PROFESSIONALS WINNER 2010

Image from Shine TV

I feel very proud to be part of this book, which represents so much of what I love about good food.

I think we have really upped our game in the Northwest over the last 20 years and you will see this in the restaurants and chefs featured, who have all been chosen for their superb ability and dedication to their craft.

Today the Northwest of England has some of the finest produce in the world, and that's no exaggeration. From Morcambe Bay cockles to Southport shrimps, from Lancashire's Bowland Beef to Wards of Birkenhead fish, Formby asparagus and Claremont farm vegetables, to name but a few. And then there's Pendrills of Chester, and you really do need to let Lancashire's cheeses speak for themselves.

The Northwest does it all and does it with world-class skill and expertise, and all in landscape that can be best described as 'stunning'. Not only is it pretty to look at, but without it there wouldn't be any of the equally stunning produce that helps to make our food so truly great.

So my point is this: fabulous surroundings and the highest quality ingredients combined with the artistry of great chefs can only have the wonderful outcome of the good, honest food you can see in this book. I personally couldn't think of anywhere else in the world I'd rather cook, and I hope that this book gives you the inspiration to try some of our best recipes for yourself.

The following pages will give you all the information you need to source the ingredients from the same places as the chefs themselves, so you can be assured of their quality and flavour.

BAKERY

BERRY FRESH BAKERY
Meadow Acre, Wrenbury Frith, Nantwich, CW5 8HN
01829 720433
www.berryfreshbakery.co.uk

Artisan produced jams, chutneys, marmalades and curds using locally grown produce wherever possible.

DEVONSHIRE BAKERY
1 High Street, Frodsham, Cheshire WA6 7AH
01928 731234
www.devonshire-bakery.co.uk

5th Generation bakers who have provided retail and wholesale bakery products to North Cheshire for over 100 years.

DOUGH 2B DIFFERENT
01254 388399
www.dough2bdifferent.co.uk

Dough 2b Different, The Artisan Bakery creates a continuously evolving range of artisan breads, seasonal desserts and patisserie.

GINGER BAKERS
Unit 6, Dockray Hall Industrial Estate, Kendal LA9 4RU
07990 541982
www.gingerbakers.co.uk

Ginger Bakers produce an inspiring array of cakes and bakes using the freshest ingredients, organic and locally sourced where possible, and always free range eggs.

GORGE' US
Gorge' Us, 7 Church Road, Bebington, Wirral CH63 7PG
01516 6448133
www.gorge-us.co.uk

Gorge'Us is a small, cosy coffee shop, situated in Bebington Village, a 5 minute walk away from the historical village of Port Sunlight, and is owned and run by Ceri Newton.

BEVERAGES

BOUTINOT
Brook House, Northenden Road, Gatley, Cheshire SK8 4DN
0161 9081300
www.boutinot.com

Boutinot is a major international wine business based in the UK. With a portfolio of over 800 wines, they are exclusive agents for around 150 producers around the world and notably, have their own wine production sites in both the northern and southern hemispheres.

D.BYRNE & CO
12 King Street, Clitheroe, Lancashire BB7 2EP
01200 423152
www.dbyrne-finewines.co.uk

D. Byrne & Co is a family owned and run award winning fine wine merchants. The family have between them over 80 years experience in the business.

DUNHAM MASSEY BREWING COMPANY
100 Oldfield Lane, Dunham
Massey, Altrincham WA14 4PE
0161 929 0663
www.dunhammasseybrewing.co.uk

Dunham Massey Brewing Company is a small family run craft brewery located on National Trust land in the town of Dunham Massey.

FRODSHAM BREWERY
Lady Heyes Craft Centre, Kingsley
Road, Frodsham, Cheshire, WA6 6SU
01928 787917
www.frodshambrewery.co.uk

Frodsham microbrewery is a small, friendly, craft based brewery and shop. Barrie and his wife Hazel run it, with assistance from Paula in sales and Ken, the drayman.

BEVERAGES

MAWSONS TRADITIONAL DRINKS
Unit 11a New Line Industrial Estate, Bacup,
Lancashire, OL13 9RW
01706 874448
www.mawsons.co.uk

*Offering sarsaparilla, dandelion and burdock and cream
soda, Mawsons is bringing back the tastes of yesteryear
using skills honed over several generations.*

PECKFORTON HILLS WATER
1 Rosebank, High Street, Tattenhall, CH3 9PR
01829 770381
www.peckforton.co.uk

*Locally sourced, bottled Cheshire spring water, from
the beautiful Peckforton hills. We are committed to
environmental sustainability and serving our customers
with the highest possible quality products.*

COOKED MEAT, PIES AND PATES

CRANSTONS QUALITY BUTCHERS
Ullswater Road, Penrith, Cumbria, CA11 7EH
01768 868680
www.cranstons.net

*Cranstons Quality Butchers was established in 1914 by
the current director's Great Uncle, Stanley Cranston, who
developed a reputation for selling the top quality meat
products in the Eden Valley from his horse and cart.*

DIGGLES LTD
56 North Road, Lancaster, Lancashire LA1 1LT
01524 62060
www.diggles.co.uk

*Diggles sell a wide range of fresh products including
traditional cooked meats and hot and cold pies.*

HOME 2 HOME DINING
78, Runcorn Rd, Moore,
Warrington, Cheshire, WA4 6TZ
01925 740561
www.home2homedining.co.uk

*Thomas and Esther produce a wide range of foods, such as
their award winning Pâté, potted beef, frozen ready meals.*

THE LANCASHIRE PASTY COMPANY
784 Whalley New Road, Blackburn, Lancashire,
BB1 9BA
01254 610895
www.lancashirepastycompany.co.uk

*After trading for 26 years as Wood's Craft Bakery, the Wood
family are now concentrating on one of their best selling
lines, The Lancashire pasty, hence their new baby The
Lancashire Pasty Company!*

THE MAFEKING BILTONG COMPANY LTD
30 Sandy Lane, Macclesfield, Cheshire, SK10 4RJ
07704 339 777
www.mafekingbiltong.co.uk

*Award-winning biltong made in Macclesfield with Cheshire
beef.*

CONFECTIONERY

CHESHIRE CHOCOLATES
22 Brookside Lane, High Lane, Stockport, Cheshire, SK6 8HL
01663 763309
www.cheshirechocolates.co.uk

Chocolates that are freshly made in small batches using the finest chocolate, imported from Belgium. Using their own ganache fillings, made with fresh fruit purees, oils and whenever possible, locally sourced ingredients.

CHOCOLATEHOUSE 1657
54 Branthwaite Brow, Kendal, Cumbria, LA9 4TX 01539 740702
www.chocolatehouse1657.co.uk

An Aladdin's cave of chocolates and gifts plus a chocolate restaurant where you can enjoy chocolate drinks, gateaux and ice creams.

KOKONOIR CHOCOLATES
41 The Boulevard, Broughton, Chester (website says Flintshire, Wales), CH4 0SN.
01244 534352
www.kokonoir.com

Jo and Toby Beevers started Kokonoir in Broughton from a shared love of how chocolates should taste. Their chocolates are all handcrafted, using traditional artisan skills to guarantee a fresh, delicious taste.

THE OLD FIRE STATION CHOCOLATE SHOP
52-54 High Street, Tarporley, Cheshire, CW6 0AG
01829 733736
www.firestationchocolateshop.co.uk

Handmade Freudenberg truffles, chocolate animals and a range of fudges are made on the premises at this old fire station in the village of Tarporley. Whatever the occasion we have chocolates to suit.

THE PASTRY KING
Alderley Road, Chelford, SK11 9AP
01565 818228
www.thepastryking.co.uk

The Pastry King is a bakery that produces fantastic quality desserts, chocolates and cakes as they are ordered. From dinner parties to wedding cakes, they can help you.

SIMON DUNN CHOCOLATIERS
Alderley Road, Wilmslow, Cheshire SK9 1JX
01625 529105
www.simondunnchocolates.co.uk

With over 25 years of experience, you can expect superb quality. All of their chocolates are made in-store by expert chocolatiers.

DAIRY

CHESHIRE FARM ICE CREAM
Drumlan Hall Farm, Newton lane, Tattenhall, Chester Cheshire, CH3 9NE
01829 770995
www.cheshirefarmicecream.co.uk

Produced on the farm, Cheshire Farm's award winning Real Dairy Ice Cream is made using fresh whole milk and fresh cream. Only the finest ingredients are carefully selected and used.

DELAMERE DAIRY
Delamere Dairy Ltd, Yew Tree Farm, Bexton Lane, Knutsford, Cheshire, WA16 9BH
01565 750528
www.delameredairy.co.uk

Roger and Liz Sutton named their dairy after Cheshire's beautiful Delamere Forest where they started their first herd with just three goats.

BURT'S CHEESE
L & M Business Park, Norman Road, Altrincham, WA14 4EP
077709 394292
www.burtscheese.com

Burt's Blue Cheese is a semi-soft blue cheese made in Altrincham, Cheshire, with quality milk sourced from a local dairy for a richer flavour. It is made in small vats, making each cheese a labour of love.

MRS KIRKHAM'S LANCASHIRE CHEESE
Beesley Farm, Mill Lane, Goosnargh, Preston. PR3 2FL
01772 865335

John Kirkham still milks the cows every day (after 30 years in business), while Ruth and son Graham still make the cheese between them, seven days a week. On sale nationally and is used in many recipes.

FARMSHOPS

CLAREMONT FARM LIMITED
Old Clatterbridge Road, Bebington, Wirral CH63 4JB

Office: 0151 334 1906
Shop: 0151 346 1796,
Kitchen: 07780 943 938
www.claremontfarm.co.uk

They tend their own land and grow crops. Wonderful farmshop and online delivery service available.

EDDISBURY FRUIT FARM
Yeld Lane, Kelsall, Cheshire, CW6 0TE
08450 941023
www.eddisbury.co.uk

Eddisbury Fruit Farm was established in 1936 by Leslie Haworth. The farm grows over 20 varieties of apples available in season for pick your own. They manufacture over 20 different single and blended varieties of apple juice using soft fruits grown on the farm.

RIVERSIDE ORGANIC
Shipbrook Hill Farm, Manor Lane,
Whatcroft, Northwich, Cheshire, CW9 7RH
01606 46258
www.riversideorganic.com

Riverside Organic is a family run farm, farm shop and cafe in Whatcroft, just out side Davenham in Cheshire. They started selling direct to the public in 2005 and boast a large range of organic produce including beef, lamb, chicken, eggs, herbs, veg and fruit. They pride themselves on producing as much food in the shop from their own farm.

FISH

FURNESS FISH & GAME
Moor Lane, Flookburgh, Grange-
over-Sands, Cumbria, LA11 7LS
01539 559544
www.morecambebayshrimps.com

A family business started by the owner Les Salisbury who has been fishing for shrimps since he was a lad, going out on the horse and cart.

SOUTHPORT POTTED SHRIMPS
66 Station Road, Banks Village,
Southport, Lancs, PR9 8BB
01704 229266
www.pottedshrimp.co.uk

Southport Potted Shrimps was founded in 1980 by James Peet, a shrimp fisherman for 25 years, whose family has been involved in the local shrimp industry for over four generations.

SOUTHPORT SEAFOODS
11 Shellfield Road, Marshside,
Southport, PR9 9US 01704 505822
www.southportseafoods.co.uk

Southport Seafoods opened in 1992 and since that date they have provided the finest quality potted shrimps which are available throughout the U.K.

MEAT

A. PICTON & SONS
Highfield Farm Shop, Waterworks
Lane, Winwick, Warrington, WA2 8TB
www.highfieldfarmshop.co.uk

Highfield farm shop produces high quality, home reared beef, lamb and pork, as well as potatoes, fruit, vegetables, eggs, jams and chutneys.

BERKINS DELI
Clitheroe Road, Barrow, Clitheroe, Lancashire BB7 9AQ
01254 821010
www.berkins.co.uk

Visit Berkins Deli adjacent to the Eagle at Barrow in the tiny village of Barrow nestled between Whalley and Clitheroe which is open seven days a week. Sells award-winning homemade sausages and 35 day aged beef.

CLARKES OF LYTHAM
Market Buildings, Lytham, Lancashire, FY8 5LS
01253 736687
www.clarkesoflytham.co.uk

Award winning Lancashire butchers, selling finest quality sausages, meat and poultry.

H CLEWLOW BUTCHERS
8 Pepper Street, Nantwich, Cheshire. CW5 5AB
01270 625366
www.clewlows.co.uk

Traditional Butchers Shop since 1929, using locally sourced, high quality stock from local farms.

THE REAL LANCASHIRE BLACK PUDDING COMPANY
Unit 4, Waterside Industrial Estate,
Haslingden, Lancashire, BB4 5EN
01706 231029
www.reallancashireblackpuddings.co.uk

The Bury Type of Black Pudding is the most favoured and considered the most traditional of all the Black Puddings.

PRESERVES, RELISHES, HONEY & PUDDINGS

ADESSO HEALTH LOVING
Unit 1, Railway Street Industrial Estate, Froxmer Street, Gorton, Greater Manchester, M188EF
0161 231 0088
www.adessofoods.co.uk

Adesso takes great pride in creating Ambient Marinades, Dips and Drizzles from only the finest ingredients.

FIND INSPIRATION IN FOOD
The Old Post Office, 1a Oak Road, Hooton, CH66 7NP
01513 273831
www.findinspirationinfood.co.uk

Homemade, luxury preserves.

PARKERS PRESERVES
Summerseat, Blackburn, Lancashire, BL9 5PN
01706 281 993
www.parkerspreserves.co.uk

Homemade, using only the freshest fruits and vegetables, with no artificial colouring , flavourings, or preservatives.

REEDY'S NATURALLY
Unit 9, Elder Court, Shadsworth Business Park, Blackburn, Lancashire BB1 2EQ
01254 691 754
www.reedys.co.uk

Delicious luxury jams, marmalades and savory condiments handmade in the heart of Lancashire.

SMOKED FOODS

THE CHESHIRE SMOKEHOUSE
Vost Farm, Morley Green, Wilmslow, Cheshire, SK9 5NU
01625 548499
www.cheshiresmokehouse.co.uk

In recent years The Cheshire Smokehouse has earned a national reputation for the quality of its range of fine foods.

PORT OF LANCASTER SMOKEHOUSE
West Quay, Glasson Dock, Lancaster, LA2 0DB
01524 752168
www.polsco.co.uk

Established over thirty years ago, the Port of Lancaster Smokehouse has retained and maintained the traditional methods of preparing and curing fish and meats of all kinds.

236
CONTRIBUTORS

3 MILLSTONES INN
Waddington Road, West Bradford, Clitheroe, Lancashire BB7 4SX
01200 443 339
www.3millstones.com

60 HOPE STREET
60 Hope Street, Liverpool L1 9BZ
0151 707 6060
www.60hopestreet.com

THE BAY HORSE INN
Bay Horse Lane, Bay Horse, Ellel, Lancaster LA2 OHR
01524 791 204
www.bayhorseinn.com

THE BUBBLE ROOM
1 Woolton Street, Liverpool L25 5NH
0151 909 4909
www.thebubbleroom.co.uk

THE DUKE OF YORK
Brow Top, Grindleton, Near Clitheroe, Lancashire BB7 4QR
01200 441 266
www.dukeofyorkgrindleton.com

THE FENCE GATE AT FENCE
Wheatley Lane Road, Fence, Nr Burnley, Lancashire
BB12 9EE
01282 618 101
www.fencegate.co.uk

FRAICHE
11 Rose Mount, Oxton, Wirral CH43 5SG
0151 652 2914
www.restaurantfraiche.com

FREEMASONS AT WISWELL
8 Vicarage Fold, Wiswell, Clitheroe, Lancashire BB7 9DF
01254 822 218
www.freemasonsatwiswell.com

THE INN AT WHITEWELL
Near Clitheroe, Lancashire BB7 3AT
01200 448 222
www.innatwhitewell.com

LA MOUETTE AT THE ROYAL HILBRE
The Royal Hilbre Boutique Hotel and Spa,
8 Meols Drive, Hoylake, Wirral CH47 4AQ
07581 263 837
www.royalhilbrehotelspa.co.uk

THE LAWNS RESTAURANT
Thornton Hall, Neston Road, Thornton Hough, Wirral CH63 1JF
0151 336 3938
www.lawnsrestaurant.co.uk

THE LONDON CARRIAGE WORKS

Hope Street, Liverpool L1 9DA
0151 705 2222
www.thelondoncarriageworks.co.uk

LUNYA

18-20 College Lane, Liverpool One, Liverpool L1 3DS
0151 706 9770
www.lunya.co.uk

MARITIME DINING ROOMS

Merseyside Maritime Museum, Albert Dock, Liverpool
L3 4AQ
0151 478 4499
www.liverpoolmuseums.org.uk

THE MONRO

92 Duke Street, Liverpool L1 5AG
0151 707 9933
www.themonro.com

PARKERS ARMS

Newton-in-Bowland, Nr Clitheroe, Lancashire BB7 3DY
01200 446 236
www.parkersarms.co.uk

PENINSULA DINING ROOM

3 Grosvenor Road, New Brighton CH45 2LW
0151 639 8338
www.peninsula-dining-room.co.uk

PUSCHKA

16 Rodney Street, Liverpool L1 2TE
0151 708 8698
www.puschka.co.uk

RHUBARB & CUSTARD

0151 932 0937
www.rhubarbandcustard.net

SALT HOUSE TAPAS

Salt House, Hanover Street L1 3DW
0151 706 0092
www.salthousetapas.co.uk

THE SIDE DOOR

29a Hope Street, Liverpool L1 9BQ
0151 707 7888
www.thesidedoor.co.uk

SPIRE

Number One, Church Road, Liverpool L15 9EA
0151 734 5040
www.spirerestaurant.co.uk

MORE QUALITY RECIPE BOOKS
AVAILABLE FROM THIS PUBLISHER

Relish North East – From the bustling city life in Newcastle, to the multitude of sleepy, rural villages, the North East has something for everyone. An introduction from the North East's best known chef, Terry Laybourne, kicks off this culinary adventure through a rich and diverse region, with many varied recipes for you to try at home including a selection from the North East's two Masterchef finalists, John Calton and David Coulson, plus many others from award-winning chefs across the region.

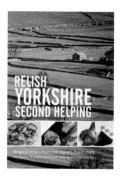

Relish Yorkshire Second Helping – The latest edition of relish Yorkshire features a foreword by celebrity chef Tessa Bramley, and returns to the county with all new recipes from Yorkshire's greatest chefs; Michelin Starred James McKenzie from The Pipe and Glass and Steve Smith from The Burlington, plus Richard Allen from The Fourth Floor at Harvey Nichols and many, many more. Relish Yorkshire: Second Helping is a must have for any hearty food lover with true Yorkshire pride.

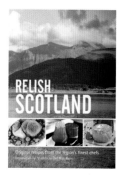

Relish Scotland – With over 300 Pages of Scotland's finest recipes, this book takes you on an epic journey from Edinburgh to Glasgow, across to Aberdeen and then up to the Highlands and Islands, through rugged landscapes and beautiful cities. An introduction from TV celebrity chef Nick Nairn prepares the palate for recipes from nationally acclaimed restaurateurs such as Tom Kitchin, Martin Wishart and Geoffrey Smeddle. With breathtaking pictures of the views and venues, Relish Scotland promises to make for fascinating reading for both foodies and tourists alike.

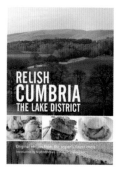

Relish Cumbria – Over 50 mouth-watering exclusive recipes for you to try at home from some of Cumbria's finest Country House Hotels and acclaimed restaurants including Nigel Mendham at The Samling, Russell Plowman at Gilpin Lodge Hotel and Andrew McGeorge at Rampsbeck Country House Hotel. Packed with innovative recipes and stunning photography to match the stunning landscape, Relish Cumbria is certain to make a fantastic addition to any cook's library.

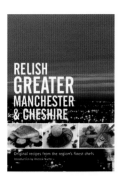

Relish Greater Manchester and Cheshire – As one of the most populated areas in the UK, Greater Manchester has a wealth of talent to display. Traditionally seen as a historic centre of industry, Manchester's finer side inspires great chefs such as Andrew Nutter and Stuart Thomson to produce truly amazing food. Alongside this, Cheshire offers a refreshing change of pace. Further away from the hustle and bustle, its own character is reflected in some equally stunning cuisine presented by Michael Caines. This Relish book shows it all in this journey around the North West.

Relish Publications – Are an independent publisher of exclusive regional recipe books, featuring only the best and brightest critically acclaimed chefs and the venues at which they work, all of which showcased with superb photography. They also work with some chefs individually to produce bespoke publications tailored to their individual specifications. Since 2009, Relish has fostered a national presence, while maintaining friendly, personalised service that their highly professional team prides themselves on.

For more information about current and future Relish books, as well as information about the chefs and restaurants featured in them, visit www.relishpublications.co.uk

RELISH
PUBLICATIONS

BOUTINOT

Proud sponsors of